THE HISTORY OF THYSSEN

THE HISTORY OF THYSSEN
Family, Industry, and Culture in the 20th Century

Günther Schulz and Margit Szöllösi-Janze

Translated by Christopher Reid

berghahn
NEW YORK • OXFORD
www.berghahnbooks.com

Published in 2023 by
Berghahn Books
www.berghahnbooks.com

English-language edition
© 2023 Berghahn Books

German-language edition
© 2021 Fritz Thyssen Stiftung

Originally published in German as
Familie – Unternehmen – Öffentlichkeit. Thyssen im 20. Jahrhundert: Ein Forschungsprojekt und sein Ertrag

All rights reserved. Except for the quotation of short passages for the purposes of criticism and review, no part of this book may be reproduced in any form or by any means, electronic or mechanical, including photocopying, recording, or any information storage and retrieval system now known or to be invented, without written permission of the publisher.

Library of Congress Cataloging-in-Publication Data

Names: Schulz, Günther, 1950– author. | Szöllösi-Janze, Margit, author.
Title: The history of Thyssen : family, industry, and culture in the 20th century / Günther Schulz and Margit Szöllösi-Janze ; translated by Christopher Reid.
Other titles: Familie - Unternehmen - Öffentlichkeit: Thyssen im 20. Jahrhundert. English
Description: New York : Berghahn Books, 2023. | Includes bibliographical references and index
Identifiers: LCCN 2022045767 (print) | LCCN 2022045768 (ebook) | ISBN 9781800739024 (hardback) | ISBN 9781800739031 (ebook)
Subjects: LCSH: Thyssen, August, 1842-1926—Family. | Thyssen & Co. (Mülheim an der Ruhr, Germany)—History. | Steel industry and trade—Germany—History—20th century. | Family-owned business enterprises—Germany—History—20th century.
Classification: LCC HD9523.9.T44 S3813 2023 (print) | LCC HD9523.9.T44 (ebook) | DDC 338.7/6691420943—dc23/eng/20220930
LC record available at https://lccn.loc.gov/2022045767
LC ebook record available at https://lccn.loc.gov/2022045768

British Library Cataloguing in Publication Data

A catalogue record for this book is available from the British Library

ISBN 978-1-80073-902-4 hardback
ISBN 978-1-80539-074-9 paperback
ISBN 978-1-80073-903-1 ebook

https://doi.org/10.3167/9781800739024

CONTENTS

The Introduction and Part I were written by Margit Szöllösi-Janze, Part II by Günther Schulz.

List of Figures	vii
Foreword to the English-Language Edition by Volker R. Berghahn	x
Foreword by Dr. Frank Suder	xvi
Introduction	1
Point of Departure: The Thyssen Legacy	1
Elements of an Entangled Family and Corporate History	4
Part I. Family History Projects: Selected Findings	9
Chapter 1. The Thyssens: Family and Fortune	11
(Simone Derix, 2016, 2nd ed. 2021)	
Family and Conflict	14
Lifestyle: Family Spaces, Local Roots, Mobility	19
"Calculated Risk": The Thyssens, Their Foundations, and Advisors	30
Chapter 2. Two Civic Lives in the Public Eye: The Brothers Fritz Thyssen and Heinrich Thyssen-Bornemisza	39
(Felix de Taillez, 2017)	
Stepping Out from the Father's Shadow: Fritz Thyssen as National Hero	40
The Exclusive Circles of Heinrich Thyssen-Bornemisza	46
Out in the Open: Fritz Thyssen, the Media, and National Socialism	53
Chapter 3. The Thyssens as Art Collectors: Investment and Symbolic Capital (1900–1970)	57
(Johannes Gramlich, 2015, 2nd ed. 2021)	
"The Bourgeois Standard Case": August Thyssen Sr. and Fritz Thyssen	59
Collecting as Vocation: Heinrich and Hans Heinrich Thyssen-Bornemisza	63

Part II. Corporate History Projects: Selected Findings   73
    Why Thyssen? On the State of Research and the Research Problem   73
    On the Company's Development   77
    Company and Family   80
    Trust—Capital—Assets   82
    Advisors and Consultants   84
    Thyssen and Thyssen-Bornemisza—Outlines of Success and Failure   87

Chapter 4. Vereinigte Stahlwerke AG under National Socialism: Corporate Policy between Market Economy and State Economy   93
(Alexander Donges, 2014)

Chapter 5. Forced Labor at Thyssen: "Stahlverein" and "Baron-Konzern" in World War II   97
(Thomas Urban, 2014, 2nd ed. 2021)

Chapter 6. The Expropriation of Fritz Thyssen: Dispossession and Restitution   103
(Jan Schleusener, 2018)

Chapter 7. Thyssen in the Adenauer Era: Corporate Formation and Family Capitalism   108
(Johannes Bähr, 2015)

Chapter 8. From Steel Group to Corporate Group: The Heinrich Thyssen-Bornemisza Companies from 1926–1932   115
(Harald Wixforth, 2019)

Chapter 9. The Thyssen-Bornemisza Group: A Transnational Business Group in Times of Economic Nationalism, 1932–1955   124
(Boris Gehlen, 2021)

Appendix. Thyssen Family Tree   129

Bibliography   132

Overview of the Book Series   136

Index   138

FIGURES

Figure 0.1. The children of August and Hedwig Thyssen (from left): Fritz, August Jr., Heinrich, and Hede, ca. 1883. Photo: Franz Erckens, Mülheim an der Ruhr (Stiftung zur Industriegeschichte Thyssen, F).   3

Figure 0.2. Amélie Thyssen as hunting mistress at Puchhof Castle hunting grounds, December 1954. Photographer unknown (thyssenkrupp Corporate Archives, F/Alb/1002). Behind her Robert Ellscheid (right), Hans-Günther Sohl (far right).   5

Figure 1.1. The Thyssen family network. The wedding of Princess Teresa zur Lippe and Hans Heinrich Thyssen-Bornemisza at Villa Favorita, Castagnola, 1 September 1946 (Stiftung zur Industriegeschichte Thyssen, F/Alb/TB/28).   12

Figure 1.2. The governess Minna Schömann and "her" children, ca. 1893, from left: August Jr., Fritz, Heinrich, and Hede Thyssen, Villa am Froschenteich in Mülheim an der Ruhr. Photographer unknown (Stiftung zur Industriegeschichte Thyssen, F).   13

Figure 1.3. August Thyssen at Landsberg Castle, Pentecost 1911. Photo: Kurt Ernst (thyssenkrupp Corporate Archives, F 4).   16

Figure 1.4. Hans Heinrich Thyssen-Bornemisza ("Heini") with Margit ("Mama") and János ("Uncle János") Wettstein von Westersheimb, 26 July 1933, photographer unknown. Postcard from Scheveningen, postmark 27 July 1933 (Stiftung zur Industriegeschichte Thyssen, F).   18

Figure 1.5. The Grandhotel as a social hub. The extended Thyssen family network at the Dunapalota Hotel (Danube Palace) in Budapest, September 1939 (from left: Adèle Bornemisza, Margit and János Wettstein von Westersheimb, Gabrielle and Adolph Bentinck van Schoonheten). Written postcard. Photographer unknown (Stiftung zur Industriegeschichte Thyssen, F/ NJT/174).   23

Figure 1.6. Heinrich Thyssen-Bornemisza (right) in Hungarian magnate costume (*díszmagyar*). On the left, probably his father-in-law and adoptive father Gábor Baron Bornemisza de Kászon in the uniform of a first lieutenant (*főhadnagy*) of the Szeged Landwehr Hussar Regiment No. 3, ca. 1910. Photographer unknown.(Stiftung zur Industriegeschichte Thyssen, F). 24

Figure 1.7. Fritz and Amélie Thyssen in Carlsbad, 1907. Photographer unknown (thyssenkrupp Corporate Archives, F/Alb/704). 28

Figure 1.8. Heinrich and Margit Thyssen-Bornemisza with their son Stephan, Carlsbad, August 1917. Photographer unknown (thyssenkrupp Corporate Archives, F/44). 29

Figure 1.9. The network of advisors around Amélie Thyssen, 17 March 1967: Kurt Birrenbach, Robert Ellscheid, Hans-Günther Sohl. Photo: Works photographer at August Thyssen-Hütte AG (thyssenkrupp Corporate Archives, F/Personen/656). 36

Figure 2.1. Trial before the French military court in the district court building in Mainz, 24 January 1923. Photo: Optische Anstalt G. A. Urmetzer Mainz. Fritz Thyssen standing in the dock, Franz Wüstenhöfer and Ernst Tengelmann seated next to him on the right. On the bench in the center, presiding judge Colonel Debeugny. At the round table r. defender Friedrich Grimm (thyssenkrupp Corporate Archives, F 422). 42

Figure 2.2. Maud Feller, c. 1933. Photo: Moseseo, Nice (Stiftung zur Industriegeschichte Thyssen, F/TB/79). 48

Figure 2.3. The "Brown Ribbon of Germany" as a media event, Munich-Riem, 26 July 1936. Photo: "Tachyphot," Franz Hoffrecht u. Sohn, Berlin. In the middle after his victory, jockey Ernst Grabsch on Nereide. At the tail end, in top hat and tailcoat, probably Heinrich Thyssen-Bornemisza (Stiftung zur Industriegeschichte Thyssen, F/TB/12/8). 51

Figure 2.4. The baron as a poster child for the National Socialists. The "Brown Ribbon of Germany," Munich-Riem, 26 July 1936, photo: "Tachyphot," Franz Hoffrecht u. Sohn, Berlin From left: Christian Weber, NSDAP floor leader in Munich city council; trainer Adrian von Borcke;

owner Heinrich Thyssen-Bornemisza (Stiftung zur Industriegeschichte
Thyssen, F/TB/12/7). 52

Figure 3.1. Amélie Thyssen in front of the painting of her late husband
Fritz in the Dreischeibenhaus ("Thyssen-Hochhaus") in Düsseldorf,
1965. Photo: Bernd König (thyssenkrupp Corporate Archives, F 431). 58

Figure 3.2. Landsberg Castle conservatory with marble sculptures
by Auguste Rodin, around 1910. Photographer unknown
(thyssenkrupp Corporate Archives, F 4042). 61

Figure 3.3. Heinrich Thyssen-Bornemisza (third from right) in
the Villa Favorita gallery, 1947. Photo: Christian Schiefer, Lugano-
Paradiso (Stiftung zur Industriegeschichte Thyssen, F). 67

Figure P2.1. Fritz Thyssen. Painting unsigned and undated, before
1926. Collotype, in: Tancred Borenius (ed.), *Haus Thyssen: Die
Sammlung* (Berlin, 1926, private print), vi (thyssenkrupp Corporate
Archives, F 424). 75

Figure P2.2. General view of August Thyssen-Hütte, 1924.
Photographer: unknown (thyssenkrupp Corporate Archives, F 1010/1). 79

Figure P2.3. Amélie Thyssen and Hans-Günther Sohl around 1960.
Photographer unknown (photo portfolio in the possession of the Fritz
Thyssen Foundation, Cologne). 85

Figure 6.1. Adolf Hitler with Fritz Thyssen (behind Hitler, right),
Albert Vögler (Vereinigte Stahlwerke AG), and Walter Borbet
(Bochumer Verein) during a plant tour in the Ruhr region on 8 April
1936. Photo: Heinrich Hoffmann (bpk Bildagentur, image 30023752). 104

Figure 7.1. French president Charles de Gaulle addresses the
workforce of August Thyssen-Hütte AG during his visit to Germany
on 6 September 1962. Photo: Günter Meyer, works photographer at
August Thyssen-Hütte AG (thyssenkrupp Corporate Archives, F 353). 112

Figure 8.1. Derby, 26 July 1936, Munich. "The Brown Ribbon of
Germany." Heinrich Thyssen-Bornemisza holds the winning horse
Nereide from his Erlenhof stud farm by the reins. Photo: Alex
Menzendorf, Berlin (Stiftung zur Industriegeschichte Thyssen,
F/TB/12/5). 121

FOREWORD TO THE ENGLISH-LANGUAGE EDITION

As a glance at the table of contents will show, this book presents a wide-ranging and ambitious agenda for research in business as well as family history. This foreword therefore begins with an explanation of why I believe that subsequent chapters are of considerable interest to both historians of international business and scholars and students working in the burgeoning field of family history. At the same time, its publication should be seen in an even wider historiographical and conceptual context of transnationality and family-owned enterprises. Both perspectives will be analyzed in more detail in this foreword.

To begin with, Günther Schulz and Margit Szöllösi-Janze's multivolume project, published in German under the title *Unternehmerfamilie Thyssen im 20. Jahrhundert*, was initiated in 2006 and funded by the Fritz Thyssen Foundation and the Stiftung zur Industriegeschichte Thyssen. Given this topic, the directors and contributors labored under a special obligation to make certain that their story did not degenerate into a hagiography but adhered to the most rigorous standards of analysis, especially as they considered such a controversial and complex subject as the history of the Thyssen family and its many industrial enterprises. What has been well-known up to the publication of the project and its concurrent digest in this book was the history of the corporation's founder August Thyssen and his son Fritz, who was a supporter and financier of Adolf Hitler and the National Socialist movement. In 1933, Fritz even accepted a nomination as a Nazi deputy in the Reichstag as well as other higher appointments in the "Third Reich."

While the widely read book *I Paid Hitler*, published in 1941, was not authenticated by him, there were other twists and turns in Fritz's life and work after he became increasingly disillusioned with the Nazi dictatorship. In 1939 he publicly broke with Hitler and fled with his wife Amélie to Switzerland and France, whereupon the regime confiscated all his assets and revoked his citizenship. Arrested by the Vichy police in 1940, he was extradited to Germany where he was put in a concentration camp until May 1945. With the victorious Allies now in control of the defeated country, Fritz Thyssen had to appear before a denazification tribunal that looked at his political record in the 1930s and fined him for his support of National Socialism. After he had made a special contribution to the restitution fund to the tune of 15 percent of his assets that could be traced in West Germany, his remaining assets were restored to him. Released from prison only after the conclusion of his trial at the end of 1948, he and his wife immigrated to Argentina where he died on 8 February 1951 at the age of seventy-seven.

Although Schulz and Szöllösi-Janze and their team of scholars were committed to providing a full analysis of these problematical aspects of Fritz Thyssen's life, his family, and his corporation in the "Third Reich," their overall approach was much broader, i.e., to undertake a case study of the type of comprehensive business-cum-family history that viewed "the allied family" as a widespread, globally acting network of all family members, including women, divorced spouses, and often forgotten siblings. Accordingly, this project can be linked to American research on kinship on which David Sabean and others have been publishing major studies, even if their work has been focused primarily on early modern Europe and the nineteenth century. The Thyssen volumes cover family affairs, marriage policies, residences, patronage, and art collections. Each of these topics has been thoroughly investigated and written up by an expert in close cooperation with the directors of the project as well as advisors and reviewers. In this sense, the history of this entrepreneurial family goes well beyond the roles of August and Fritz Thyssen and is much more comprehensive than earlier research that dealt with their coal, iron, and steel corporations in the Ruhr region.

Given the range of the Thyssen project, its contributors had the opportunity to evaluate hitherto unexploited sources, including some held in American archives. They also related to Fritz Thyssen's brother Heinrich Thyssen-Bornemisza, his widely branched family line, and his international holding company that pursued its own, separate business strategies. This TB Group emerged from a division of the August Thyssen inheritance implemented between 1927 and 1936 and predominantly comprised the non-steel parts of the Thyssen empire abroad. Initially, the group's interests revolved around energy, raw materials, trade, and, above all, the banking sector. Later it shifted its business activities even more strongly toward international trade and finance and further reduced its participations in domestic industries after World War II. This meant that the TB Group was transformed from a family enterprise engaged in production to a *portfolio business group* that continues to operate very successfully to this day. It is very much a decentralized conglomerate, delivering clear management decisions and focusing on output-related compensation. It also adheres to strict accounting practices, and all this means more generally that the group offers many lessons that are of interest to the development of modern management practices.

It is therefore not only the many insights and academic stimuli that this project provides for business historians in the English-speaking world who are interested in the history of individual Thyssen enterprises; at the same time there are important, more comprehensive lessons to be learned from the evolution of both the Thyssen and Thyssen-Bornemisza conglomerates. Three major aspects should be highlighted here. To begin with, there is the question of how success was secured through diversification into the raw materials sector, industrial production, credit, trade, and services. These were the keys to Thyssen's success. Secondly, there was the quest to secure the family enterprise through an engagement in the international global economy, which often required having to cope with different political regimes. In this respect, Thyssen's and Thyssen-Bornemisza's interests in Switzerland (by means of foundations), Britain, and other European states, but also in the United States and Latin America, played an important role. Thirdly, there was the specific connection between family and enterprise, especially in management and asset management. Thus, the influence of managers, lawyers, and consultants was considerable, while there were also complex legal arrangements relating to inheritance agreements among heirs and their monetary compensation.

In the end, the project comprised ten volumes that appeared between 2014 and 2021, published by Schöningh/Brill in Paderborn. The two directors of the project then decided to provide a more accessible digest of the family-focused volumes, on the one hand, and the entrepreneurial volumes, on the other. This digest in turn became the basis of this translation into English, given that it was even less practical to translate all volumes into English. It is thus the hope that this book will enable interested scholars and graduate students to learn about how the larger project was conceptualized and executed and what new perspectives are being offered in it.

However, the Thyssen project should be linked to the work of the German Historical Institute in Washington that Hartmut Berghoff started in 2010, when he became the director of the GHI in Washington, whose mission is to promote transatlantic and now also transpacific academic exchanges, dialogs, conferences, and research projects. Soon after his arrival, Berghoff launched a biographical, multigenerational study of over three hundred German-American businessmen and their families. In this respect the GHI project was quite different from the Thyssen one. It is against this background that I shall now try to build a bridge between the latter and the no less ambitious project that Berghoff and his colleagues started at the GHI between 2010 and 2016. Being an internationally renowned economic and business historian and responding to the then-growing interest in transnational migration, the GHI began to study the life and work of immigrants from Central Europe who established businesses all over the United States. Unlike the Thyssen study of a large single family, this project had to begin with a statistical record and identify a large number of immigrants from Central Europe who became business families. Accordingly, the GHI began to collect their biographies. An estimated sixteen million Europeans came to the United States in several waves, of whom some 30 percent came from Central Europe. Accordingly, Berghoff's team scoured a large number of sources to compile relevant biographical data to be woven into narrative entries. These were then carefully peer-reviewed and, once finalized, made accessible on a searchable GHI website.

What makes this website additionally valuable to researchers is that, apart from those biographical entries, it includes images/photos as well as key documents and bibliographical references. Critical of the "one-dimensional functionalism" of some approaches to business history, Berghoff also aimed from the start to "reintegrate into business history the entrepreneurs' values and beliefs, motivations of leadership, family influences, private networks, and employees, and reputation and 'trust,'" as highlighted, for example, also by the French business historian Patrick Fridenson and his American colleague Philip Scranton. As the sources for these topics were assembled, the role of women in these families also received special attention.

The early findings of this project were discussed at an international conference in June 2016 and subsequently published in a supplement of the *Bulletin* of the GHI where the summaries can be consulted, also raising such methodological questions as assembling a sample that could claim to be representative. Another problem was the lack of similar studies to enable comparison. The findings of the GHI project are now available on the GHI website under the title "Immigrant Entrepreneurship: German-American Business Biographies 1720 to the Present," divided into five volumes: I. 1720–1840; II. 1840–1893; III. 1893–1918; IV. 1918–1945; V. 1945 to Present. Given the range of topics that the GHI project is covering, Berghoff and his team, following the approach of the anthropologist Clifford Geertz, were concerned to provide, as far as possible, "thick descriptions" of their subjects, but were also conscious, like Schulz and Szöllösi-Janze, that it was imperative not to lapse into hagiography.

While the table of contents of the Thyssen project should be held against the range of socioeconomic, political, cultural, and ideological topics of the GHI project, there is yet another approach that has more recently been developed in the study of socioeconomic and cultural history. If the Thyssen project revolves around an all-inclusive analysis of a major German steel corporation as well as the TB Group, its publication should also be seen in the context of an adjacent field of research that is concerned with medium-sized and small business firms in which there has been a growing interest. Whereas the big corporations were at the center of scholarship in earlier decades, resulting in important studies of the publicly traded shareholding corporations, their governance and management, as well as their operations in domestic and international markets, the small and medium-sized firms tend to be family owned and, if not directed by members of the family, at least decisively influenced by them. In the German context, it was the Chicago University historian and social scientist Gary Herrigel who published two important books and many articles on these Mittelstand enterprises in postwar Germany. More recently, Hartmut Berghoff and Ingo Köhler have added their comparative work on family firms in a volume titled *Verdienst und Vermächtnis: Familienunternehmen in Deutschland und in den USA seit 1800*, which, while focused on changes in structures and institutional frameworks as well as corporate governance, also broaches such topics as historical origins, shifts, and path dependencies. The two authors also look at laws of inheritance, business paternalism, the role of women, and cultural identities, while always bearing in mind the similarities but also the differences between the United States and Germany. The book finally contains some fascinating comparisons between traditions of German quality production and American mass production.

In short, the two authors examine topics on which a growing number of more detailed case studies have meanwhile also been completed. Keeping the focus on German research, the perhaps most important shift occurred, starting from Herrigel, in the movement of the center of gravity in German industry from the Rhineland and the heavy industrial corporations of the Ruhr region to regions in the south and southwest, where one finds industries of the Second Industrial Revolution of electrical engineering, chemicals, and manufacturing engineering. While the Ruhr fell behind, it was Daimler and Bosch in Stuttgart, BMW in Munich, and Audi in Ingolstadt, as well as the chemical corporations BASF, Hoechst, and Bayer along the Rhine from Leverkusen to Mannheim-Ludwigshafen, that were the most successful enterprises both at home and in the world market. However, they could hardly have been as successful without the dynamism of the Mittelstand enterprises, which were very often family managed or at least family influenced and open to technological innovation. It is no coincidence that the Münster University historian Michael Prinz has spoken of the "Württembergization" of German industry. Mention must in this context also be made of Christina Lubinski, Jeffrey Fear, and Paloma Fernández Pérez, who edited in 2013 a collection of essays under the title *Family Multinationals: Entrepreneurship, Governance and Pathways to Internationalization*. This volume includes studies on Feltrinelli, Bertelsmann, Pat'a, and Du Pont in the nineteenth century. Fear played a major role in Berghoff's GHI project, and Berghoff in turn contributed to the Lubinski/Fear/Pérez anthology.

I hope it has become clear in these few paragraphs why Hartmut Berghoff's GHI project, the studies on medium-sized family enterprises by Herrigel and Prinz, and the book on the Thyssen family, its branches, and its sprawling businesses may be of interest to a larger readership in the

English-speaking world, those involved in the rich fields of business as well as family history and who wrestle with the difficult question of how the two genres might be combined in new and insightful ways.

—Volker R. Berghahn

FOREWORD

It all started with an abundance of new sources. In 2006, Georg Heinrich Thyssen-Bornemisza, a great-grandson of August Thyssen, established the Stiftung zur Industriegeschichte Thyssen together with the thyssenkrupp Group. This Duisburg-based nonprofit foundation for the promotion of science and research set out to bring together archives from the Thyssen-Bornemisza family, thyssenkrupp AG, and other industrial historical sources and make them accessible to research. The largest part of the archive material, now running to around twenty-five linear meters of shelving, is the "Thyssen-Bornemisza" collection. In addition to company files, it also includes a sizeable number of family documents and records relating to the art collection. Along with the documents of the former Thyssen AG and its predecessor companies preserved in the thyssenkrupp Corporate Archives, the collection of sources expanded significantly. Now, it was possible to conduct new and intensive research into the history of one of the most important, globally networked industrial families of the twentieth century.

The Fritz Thyssen Stiftung took the opportunity to launch the historical research project "Unternehmerfamilie Thyssen im 20. Jahrhundert" ("The Thyssen Entrepreneurial Family in the Twentieth Century"). After a series of preliminary discussions, Prof. Dr. Christoph Buchheim (Seminar for Economic and Social History, University of Mannheim) and Prof. Dr. Margit Szöllösi-Janze (Department of History, University of Cologne, since 2010 Ludwig-Maximilians-Universität Munich) developed an overall concept that was unveiled in 2009. The project was divided into a family history and a corporate-history section with initially seven and later nine monographic studies. Prof. Dr. Szöllösi-Janze (family history) and Prof. Dr. Buchheim (corporate history) jointly headed the research network that emerged; after the latter's untimely death in December 2009, Prof. Dr. Günther Schulz (Institute of Historical Studies, Rheinische Friedrich-Wilhelms-Universität Bonn) took charge of the corporate history research team. This was supplemented by a study on the history of the founding of the Fritz Thyssen Foundation, written by Prof. Dr. Hans Günter Hockerts (History Department, Ludwig-Maximilians-Universität Munich), who also contributed to the project as an advisor.

The research project was funded in equal parts by the Fritz Thyssen Stiftung and the Stiftung zur Industriegeschichte Thyssen. It was further conceived and carried out by the network of participating historians, who enjoyed total scholarly freedom. Several internal workshops were supplemented by larger public meetings. A kickoff event, which took place 27–29 October 2010 at the Historisches Kolleg in Munich, presented the basic structure of the undertaking as well as the methodological approaches of the individual projects to an audience of experts. Key findings, summarized in an interdisciplinary manner, were reported by the research group at an international conference that brought together more than two hundred experts from a range of academic disciplines at the Berlin-Brandenburg Academy of Sciences and Humanities, 23–25 June 2014. The respective monographs—ten volumes, four of which are already in their second edition—were published in the series Familie – Unternehmen – Öffentlichkeit edited by Hans Günter Hockerts, Günther Schulz, and Margit Szöllösi-Janze, and published by Verlag Ferdinand Schöningh, Paderborn, an imprint of the Brill Group.

The report from the project managers presented below sheds light on an unusually fruitful research project, one that also produced a number of graduate and postgraduate theses. While the greatly expanded source material formed the backbone of the research, the research network also included and evaluated many other holdings in archives, both within and outside of Europe. This reflects the kind of transnationality that has characterized the Thyssen family and business history since the end of the nineteenth century.

Now that the project is completed, I welcome the opportunity to express my sincere gratitude to the project managers of the research network "Unternehmerfamilie Thyssen im 20. Jahrhundert," Prof. Dr. Margit Szöllösi-Janze and Prof. Dr. Günther Schulz. I also wish to extend my thanks to Prof. Dr. Hans Günter Hockerts as co-editor of this series of publications for the many years of intensive discussion and tireless support of the individual research projects. Special thanks are due to Prof. Dr. Manfred Rasch, who, as head of the thyssenkrupp Corporate Archives and director of the Stiftung zur Industriegeschichte Thyssen, has always provided, along with his team, active support for the indexing of the two archive collections and assisted the project in fruitful discussions. Finally, I would like to thank Georg Heinrich Thyssen-Bornemisza in particular. In establishing the Stiftung zur Industriegeschichte Thyssen he provided the initial impetus for this research project.

—Dr. Frank Suder, Director of the Fritz Thyssen Stiftung

INTRODUCTION

Who were the Thyssens? The research network "Die Unternehmerfamilie Thyssen im 20. Jahrhundert" (The Thyssen Family of Entrepreneurs in the Twentieth Century) took this question literally, placing it at the center of its investigation. According to the academic literature, entrepreneurial families combine two sets of strategies: an entrepreneurial one, aimed at achieving optimal market success, and a family-based one, geared toward securing succession and keeping the company in the family's possession over the long term. As a result, the two strategies have historically given rise to a specific family and corporate culture that differs from purely managerial companies.

The research network faced the special challenge of bringing together and integrating company and family history, which had been treated as separate historical subdisciplines. After all, separating the two strands can only relate the story of the Thyssens in a reductive way. But where are the interconnections between the crisis-ridden families and the equally turbulent corporate history of Thyssen to be found, especially when they are woven into the extended timeline from the end of the nineteenth century to the 1970s? Unlike any other time in German and European history, there were rapid and radical changes of political systems between monarchy, democracy, and dictatorship, severe economic and social crises, and death and destruction resulting from two world wars. Yet there were also new beginnings and spurts of social and cultural modernization. All of this had a massive impact on the Thyssen family and its businesses, which were part of these developments and actively influenced them.

Nonetheless, the history of the Thyssens was also determined by their peculiar rhythms and ruptures, which stemmed from internal family causes and followed typical Thyssen trajectories.

Point of Departure: The Thyssen Legacy

The research network decided that its overarching theme, which frames the individual projects, should be the legacy of the company's founder August Thyssen. This approach, however, entailed something peculiar to the Thyssens, for the question of succession did not arise with the death of the patriarch, who died on Easter Sunday, 4 April 1926, at Landsberg Castle south of

Essen and Mülheim. The analysis rather needed to begin a good four decades earlier, in December 1885, with August's divorce from his wife Hedwig, née Pelzer. The circumstances of the split were rather unusual.

After the marriage, August had fully invested his wife's considerable dowry into building up his company. As the couple lived in joint property, Hedwig could claim all the assets gained during the thirteen-year marriage in the divorce proceedings, including those tied up in the business ventures. The immediate goal of the company founder was to prevent it from being broken up. To pay off his wife, he would have had to dissolve the enterprise. He therefore explored other avenues with the help of a notary. Less than a year before the divorce was finalized, the two parties to the dispute concluded an agreement on 15 January 1885, in the presence of August's brother and partner Joseph Thyssen and a legal representative of the four children, Fritz, August, Heinrich, and Hedwig, who were still minors. They agreed to resolve and stipulate all management, succession, and property matters affected by the couple's planned separation. The divorce agreement thus coincided with the settlement of August Thyssen's vast inheritance. It set the company's course of succession, but it also cast a shadow over the entire family for four decades, until the patriarch's death.[1]

In the simplest part of the agreement, Hedwig waived her claims in favor of a lifetime allowance. Regarding the children, however, the still-married couple agreed on a provision whose far-reaching consequences they probably couldn't foresee when the contract was signed. They transferred "all their jointly owned property to the four children from their marriage ... for full and unrestricted ownership." In other words, it was an *inter vivos* inheritance. But the decisive factor for its implementation was that the children, who were initially treated equally, were the owners and yet massively restricted in the use of their property rights. August reserved for himself, secured by a notary public, "the exclusive power of disposition, administration and bond-free usufruct for life," so that "without his permission the children (would) not be authorized to dispose of the transferred property."[2]

Divorce was uncommon at the time and a fundamentally stigmatizing decision in society—even more so for a Catholic like August Thyssen. It visibly and contractually broke with the prevailing bourgeois family norm of the loving cohabitation of father, mother, and minor children in a common household. It was also the prelude to an early, decades-long succession crisis over August Thyssen's numerous enterprises, over management claims and codetermination rights, over a lot of money, and over prestige and rank in the family hierarchy, where the company's authoritarian founder claimed his place at the top. The separation of the parents was therefore the beginning of a permanent conflict that was to last for decades—a conflict in which several lines of deep division in the family intersected and mutually reinforced each

Figure 0.1. The children of August and Hedwig Thyssen (from left): Fritz, August Jr., Heinrich, and Hede, ca. 1883. Photo: Franz Erckens, Mülheim an der Ruhr.

other. Only before his death did August look back on his life self-critically: "Our divorce," he confessed frankly to his former wife Hedwig, was "a terrible misfortune for our children." The agreements from 1885 had "caused so much mischief" that he now felt "the urgent need to make up for the resulting damage."[3] Forty years on, however, it was too late.

Elements of an Entangled Family and Corporate History

One central historical element that brings together family and corporate history is, first and foremost, the notion of "wealth" (*Vermögen*), which is understandably referred to in the divorce agreement. The research network decided to follow Simone Derix, whose study conceptually unites the individual studies in many respects, and to use the source term of *fortune* as an analytical concept. Fortune comes in various forms, its composition is diverse and changes over time, and it offers the wealthy "agency", that is the potential to act or, even more so, the power to act. If family and fortune are thought of together conceptually, there are manifold implications and consequences.[4]

The many companies—while certainly important—were just one part of Thyssen's fortune. The term also includes numerous other kinds of wealth that need to be correlated: from investments in companies, corporations and holdings, funds, and monetary and fixed assets to real estate, hunting and agricultural estates, racehorses, precious jewelry, extensive collections of paintings, and other works of art. Typical of the Thyssens was how they contributed their affluence to numerous foundations, although the purpose of the endowments varied. Fortune goes beyond material goods. It also includes socially institutionalized opportunities to act, i.e., the resource known as "social capital,"[5] which is based on exclusive membership to a social group (e.g., nobility, family, elite schools, or clubs) and its dense network of the "best" connections. Undoubtedly, implicit prestige, the intimate knowledge of the "rules" and functioning mechanisms of the group, and institutionalized courses of action can correspond to monetary value. The same applies, for example, to the "cultural capital" of an art collection, which partly determines its value for the owner beyond that of a mere capital investment.

The juggling of different types of assets, the frequent transfers of wealth from one form of investment to another, was supposed to exemplify the lifestyle of the ultra-rich family, their management of conflicts, their conspicuous entrepreneurial activity, and their unusual financial dealings. Second, in this context, the research network became increasingly aware of the urgent need to systematically include the category of gender as a social construct in its analyses. The Thyssens' history makes it abundantly clear that access to, transfer of, and disposal of wealth were regulated by gender in legal, social, and everyday practical terms. In this highly exclusive, ultra-rich family, the women had fundamentally different opportunities to act than the male members. This was laid out already in the upbringing of the sons and daughters and continued in the administration of allowances, alimony and settlements, dispositions, and bequests. Across the generations, only the men were able to be operationally active at the top of the various companies. As for who would succeed as the company head and family patriarch, it was subject to negotiation according to the unwritten rules of the time. The situation could diverge, however, as in the case of Amélie Thyssen. Here, the wife was in possession of considerable stock assets after the death of her husband Fritz, which she was able to leverage with the support of advisors.

Third, the huge fortune of an ultra-rich family, dispersed according to its various forms and investments, is fundamentally under threat. It must be protected, defended, removed from the clutches of third parties, and ideally increased. It is also to be distributed among the individual members of the family—a highly complex undertaking in which by no means only the male heads of the company were involved, but the entire family network.[6] This aspect also merged family and corporate history and sheds light on a whole array of strategies to safeguard assets that were constantly perceived to be at risk. For example, threats included government intervention, taxation and expropriation, revolution, economic crises, and war. But there was also a need to protect against dangers caused to a certain extent within the family because of unclear inheritance provisions, divorce claims, or escalating quarrels.

These safeguarding strategies included the early global diversification of assets in the manner of an internationalization of capital, but also cam-

Figure 0.2. Amélie Thyssen as hunting mistress at Puchhof Castle hunting grounds, December 1954. Photographer unknown. Behind her Robert Ellscheid (right), Hans-Günther Sohl (far right). As a rule, women were not admitted to hunting parties, which served to cultivate business as well as social ties.

ouflaging them against outsiders and investing them in innocently named foundations at home and abroad, e.g., Germany and the Netherlands, and above all Switzerland. It is here that the intricate web of Thyssen foundations becomes visible. In general, they were able to fulfill a wide range of functions, especially to benefit or provide for family members, to manage assets and shareholdings, and to control holding companies, individual companies, and supervisory boards. Apart from the Thyssens, foundations are also known from the Siemens and Krupp families. However, to date, they have barely been studied historically—which is hardly surprising. Family foundations prefer to operate discreetly and tend to avoid leaving publicly accessible records. On this score, the Thyssen research group encountered remarkably favorable research conditions.

Fourth, this observation highlights the prominent role always played by the numerous trusted advisors in the Thyssens' close circle, who provided their expert knowledge to the family in the various European countries. In the words of cultural historian Thomas Macho, modernity in general was an "epoch of metastasizing consultation needs and offers," and advising was its "hallmark."[7] The research network encountered the social figure of the expert, all too familiar today, in the form of the Thyssens' numerous legal and financial advisors. They accompanied the individual family members through the almost permanent legal disputes within the family, be it property conflicts in the context of divorces, be it inheritances or attempted disinheritances. However, a wide network of advisors was also employed for the purpose of securing and increasing assets, even in the absence of a specific dispute. Thus, there were the art experts who assisted the Thyssens when they invested considerable sums to acquire works of art. Other advisors specialized in the intricacies of asset distribution or the various ways of accessing family assets, as practiced by the numerous Thyssen foundations. Did the Thyssens, the research network inquired, have a family-specific advising culture?

The influence, effectiveness, and impact of the consultants and advisors around the Thyssens resulted from the fact that individual personalities entered long-standing, highly personalized, sometimes even intimate positions of trust. Besides their expertise and experience, trust that had been proven over the course of a lifetime was a critical asset for their role as counselors. The research group repeatedly noted how the family through its network of closely connected advisors extended beyond the core family, related by blood and marriage. The family effectively pushed its boundaries outward, with the scope of advisor networks varying over time and political regimes, but always stretching into business, culture, and politics.

In this context, family and corporate history projects faced extremely complex consulting scenarios. The related constellations illuminate the delicate position of the Thyssen advisors in the decision-making processes. A consulting relationship is inherently marked by asymmetries of power. The person seeking counsel loses competence to act due to their own lack of knowledge and places him- or herself in a dependent position; for his part, an ambitious advisor can pursue his own interests. Conversely, if the advisor squanders the trust of the principal, he can lose his powerful position overnight, if with a generous payoff. The research network discovered vivid examples of both extremes.

As Derix points out, the advisors could rise to the rank of virtual Thyssen family members due to their intimate knowledge of the family's highly complex financial and private circumstances. Their familiarity with the very different legal systems of the countries of Europe and the complicated interweaving of assets, legal relationships, and personal constellations permitted them to offer financial, legal, and everyday assistance, even in the frequent intrafamily conflicts. They acted as mediators, intervening to arbitrate and negotiate workable solutions. Thus, many decisions, recommendations, and proposed resolutions to conflicts resulted from multilayered negotiation processes: between the individual advisors, between the advisors and the advised. The latter included the Thyssen women, who were especially dependent on expert counsel. Of course, in the worst case, trust could turn into dependence, proving that preserving, increasing, and safeguarding family wealth is always a precarious balancing act.

Fifth, these insights persuaded the research network that it would be inaccurate to view the Thyssens, as was long the case, as a German entrepreneurial family in the coal-iron-steel sector with deep roots in the Ruhr region.[8] This was not entirely wrong, as most research has focused on August Sr. and Fritz. In the end, however, the Thyssens were a family network with remarkable early global reach and international entanglements. They were moreover highly mobile, moving about Europe and the world according to economically and socially determined rhythms in both their business and private affairs. From visits to fashionable spas and seaside resorts, stays in the trendy grand hotels and sanatoriums to the hunting, horse racing, and, ball seasons—the Thyssens were an integral part of ultra-rich and aristocratic milieus in Europe and to some extent of the period's high society. The geographic network of intra- and interfamilial, but also entrepreneurial and financial, relationships expanded so rapidly that the Thyssens presented themselves as a transnational family already by the end of the nineteenth century. Thus, the choice and, if necessary, change of nationality were likewise subject to deliberate decision-making and negotiation, as was the temporary or permanent belonging to a particular region. Crossing national borders was part of the family's day-to-day experience and business activity.

Notes

1. Here as for the following, unless otherwise stated: Derix, *Die Thyssens*, 237–39; Lesczenski, *August Thyssen*, 59, 79–84.
2. Quoted from Lesczenski, *August Thyssen*, 81f.
3. Quoted from ibid., 85f.; cf. also August Thyssen to Hedwig de Neuter, 18 July 1925, in Rasch, *Briefe*, 395.
4. On this subject in detail, Derix, *Die Thyssens*, 14–28.
5. Cf. Bourdieu, *Mechanismen*, 63.
6. See Derix, *Die Thyssens*, 323–78; cf. also the results of the family history projects in detail.
7. Macho, "Einleitung," 29.
8. Cf. Derix, *Die Thyssens*, 29–38; similarly Gehlen, *Thyssen-Bornemisza-Gruppe*, 14f.

PART I

FAMILY HISTORY PROJECTS
SELECTED FINDINGS

CHAPTER 1

THE THYSSENS
FAMILY AND FORTUNE

(Simone Derix, 2016, 2nd ed. 2021)

The studies of family history within the research project were based on a conceptual approach that did not blindly reproduce common assumptions about family or hastily lead to a reconstruction of the biographies of the patriarchal "heads of the family," that is the few well-known men of the core Thyssen family. The study of Simone Derix, conceived as an overarching project that illuminates a broad range of themes, explores a different approach by understanding family as a family network.[1] A network conceptually is a web of relations in which there is no a priori fixed inside and outside, no top and bottom, and no distinction between a central and a marginal position. Such determinations and attributions are made only, as the case may be, during concrete empirical investigation.

Furthermore, a network fundamentally crosses borders, i.e., it can link up with other networks via corresponding vertices. It further implies that there is a spatial dimension in that it makes visible affiliations and absences, structural patterns, and relational orders. Above all, a network always reflects a dynamic process of change over time. Although it can remain stable over longer phases, it is, however, in principle in a permanent state of flux: A network can unravel and reconstitute itself, shrink and expand; it can spin off elements and reintegrate them.

Viewing the Thyssen family history as a network has many implications. In the first place, Derix's study can link the two independent studies by Felix de Taillez on the brothers Fritz and Heinrich Thyssen(-Bornemisza) and Johannes Gramlich on the Thyssens as art collectors under a common concept. Furthermore, Derix's book establishes a variety of links to the corporate history projects by systematically inquiring into the connection between economic and personal relationships.

An understanding of family as a network accomplishes even more. First, the female members of the family are of course included in the study from the very beginning; in terms of relevance, women are not relegated to the

Figure 1.1. The Thyssens as a family network. The wedding of Princess Teresa zur Lippe and Hans Heinrich Thyssen-Bornemisza at Villa Favorita, Castagnola, 1 September 1946.²

fringe. This proved even more important as there were several high-profile Thyssen women, whether born, married, or divorced, who acted with striking autonomy for their generation and who forged their own networks. Second, the family history studies did not simply reproduce superficial divisions into main and secondary family lines, patriarchs who set the tone and "black sheep," but addressed and historicized such classifications. Third, the analysis also included trusted persons who lived and acted in close contact with the family. In addition to the advisors mentioned above, such as lawyers, financial consultants, or managing directors, it was above all the service personnel (governess, cook, chauffeur, butler, tutor) who could de facto fill the function of a "surrogate family" for the children for years. Domestic servants formed the "logistical infrastructure" that made the lifestyles of their masters possible.³ The close friends belonging to social milieus such as the international communities of aristocrats and diplomats, in which individual Thyssen family members liked to move, could also be part of "family" in a broader sense. In other words, the Thyssen family noticeably spread out, linking itself with other family networks. Fourth, this approach also highlighted the entrepreneurial family as a dynastic narrative, that is as a temporal construct that extends into the past and the future. August Sr. already put into practice his own commemorative policy. After his death, and increasingly again in the early Federal Republic, the Thyssens developed a historical self-interpretation as a full-fledged family dynasty, starting from the idealized founder figure and encompassing not only the living but also the deceased and future company and family heads.[4] Fifth, a concept of family as network offers a starting point for analyzing international history as a historical subdiscipline differently, namely, in terms of transnational expansion. Families like the Thyssens operated across national borders, but they always faced the challenge of having to deal with nation-states and their national interests, institutions, legislation, and policies.[5]

Focusing on the family's handling of its fortune, Simone Derix addresses the intergenerational practices, patterns of behavior, dwelling forms, and ways of life of the Thyssens in the twentieth century. Historians called it "[a]n empirically dense and methodologically well-thought-out monograph, which opens up a new field of research in an exemplary manner."[6] The study was consequently awarded the Carl Erdmann Prize by the German Historical Association in 2016. Derix's findings and insights inform historical research on wealth, which has only recently begun to gain a foothold in international

Figure 1.2. The governess Minna Schömann and "her" children, ca. 1893, from left: August Jr., Fritz, Heinrich, and Hede Thyssen, Villa am Froschenteich in Mülheim an der Ruhr. Photographer unknown.

historical scholarship and has numerous cross-disciplinary connections to fields such as sociology, ethnology, and cultural studies. Although still in its infancy, one thing has become clear beyond the Thyssens: the family network constituted the "central site of resource formation," including the generation and transmission of relevant knowledge and experience, shared values, and a "collective sense of profit."[7] Family assets were "secured in complex wealth structures, which in all cases were tied to the family and became internationalized at an early stage." According to Gajek and Kurr, this unequivocal finding for the first half of the twentieth century should also be explored for the period after World War II, when family structures changed radically.[8]

Derix analyzed the Thyssen family history, drawing on sources from thirty-six archives in Germany and abroad, along multiple interpretational axes. From the abundance of new findings and insights, only a few, but particularly vivid examples are selected in the following to illustrate the achievements of the research project. This final report is also intended to encourage readers to pick up the monographs, and delve into the colorful details of the study's findings.

Family and Conflict

One central line of interpretation is represented by the numerous conflicts in the family, whose epicenter was the turmoil surrounding "the inheritance" triggered by August's divorce from Hedwig. For decades, the Thyssens' "normal state of affairs" was conflict—the numerous divorced marriages, the inheritance disputes and court cases, the damaged or even destroyed family relationships both between and within generations. There were notable exceptions, such as the fifty-year-long harmonious marriage of Fritz and Amélie Thyssen. And there were countervailing, inclusive mechanisms that secured the family as well as the company, such as adoptions, inheritances, and divisions of estates, and, more generally, the education of daughters and sons, which will be discussed later. Nevertheless, according to Derix's hypothesis and conclusion, the Thyssen family functioned over generations through mechanisms of conflict and exclusion: through financial disentanglements, divorce, or payoffs, through spatial distancing, but also through publicly escalating spirals of conflict, media scandals, and court cases. It was not uncommon for the Thyssens to go to extremes, such as pathologizing deviant behavior or attempting incapacitation and disinheritance procedures. For decades, their family ties were deeply marked by disappointment, competition, distrust, and strife. In their time, the Thyssens represented a veritable "anti-family."

Conflict thus gains its rightful place in genealogy and family history. The case of the Thyssens shows that what bound the family members together deeply and permanently were not the positive emotions of love and affection but the fierce disputes over wealth. To put a finer point on it: conflict did not destroy the family but shaped it—with all the associated effects on the internal emotional climate and the negative psychological strain on individual family members.

The perpetual conflict with the father, which was agonizing for everyone, may have been intensified by the fact that he was a self-confident and belligerent patriarch, but essentially crippled in his authority. While headstrong and short-tempered, August Sr. was of small stature. At 1.58 meters, he did not meet the contemporary manly ideal. In Wilhelminian times, it was said that "a German man must cast shadows." There were also other underlying deficits that served to weaken his standing as a man and company director. Not only the divorce from his wife but also their more intimate circumstances were a barely concealed scandal. Hedwig Thyssen had traveled alone for years to chic spas and resorts and engaged into romantic liaisons. She was therefore responsible for audible murmurs about August's biological paternity in the case of their common daughter Hedwig ("Hede").[9] The breach of norms by a woman was particularly grave from a social point of view. Likely, it was August who filed for divorce with the Duisburg Regional Court, citing his wife's adultery as the reason.[10] The fact that custody of the four minor children rested with the father, however, was up to the period's unquestioned patriarchal understanding of family law.[11]

August Thyssen thus broke with the hegemonic bourgeois family model of his time in several respects: The successful company founder was both a cuckold and a divorced Catholic in an environment of predominantly Protestant entrepreneurs. He was the head of an imperfect family, maintaining several nonmarital relationships himself, some in secret, others thinly disguised from the local public. Although he thereby formally adhered to the Catholic Church's ban on remarriage, he also demonstrated the double standard among the bourgeoisie. As Thomas Nipperdey put it, society distinguished "between a male and a female morality" while tolerating "a hidden way of life for men."[12]

Simone Derix's vivid study shows how the Thyssen sons Fritz, August Jr., and Heinrich were profoundly influenced by the constant drudgery of the patriarchal, controlling father figure and how, as they grew older, they pressed for an expansion of their rights and means of control. They found themselves subjected to a decades-long probationary period in which they sought to prove their leadership qualities to their father and wrest joint decision-making rights in order to be recognized as grown men and corporate leaders. They were not only in constant conflict with their father but—

Figure 1.3. August Thyssen at Landsberg Castle, Pentecost 1911. Photo: Kurt Ernst (thyssenkrupp Corporate Archives, F 4).

on the flip side of the coin—also in constant competition with each other. Conversely, August Sr. considered himself indispensable, as he did not trust any of his sons to take his place and responsibly run the corporate group. He charged them with "completing the half-finished work" of building the company but feared that they would "destroy" it instead.[13] The sense that his legacy was under threat was a daily reality for the company's founder.

August Sr. alternately saw himself being contested or courted by each of his sons. Yet, in hindsight, it becomes clear that changing constellations and partnerships of conflict emerged over the decades: the mother versus the father, all siblings and the mother versus the father, the father and one son versus the other sons, the father in an attempted alliance with his nephews Julius and Hans versus his sons. A generation later, the conflicting constellations recurred to some extent, as in the case of Fritz Thyssen's widow Amélie and her lasting tensions with daughter Anita and the two grandsons in South America. As Hockerts's study of the beginnings of the Fritz Thyssen Foundation shows, Amélie struck the grandchildren from her will. The half of the inheritance originally intended for them was earmarked for the as-yet-unfounded Fritz Thyssen Foundation. Although Anita was appointed sole heir, the company's property was reduced by almost half through the act of endowment.[14] All parties involved, the research network found, exhibited individual "styles of fighting".

The patterns of conflict are multifaceted and fluctuating, of course, for reconciliations also occurred repeatedly. That said, they were often followed by a reconfiguration of alliances in a re-escalating conflict. The socialization of daughters and sons, who were always taught all-encompassing ideas of order, behavioral norms, and values in addition to their formal education, was certainly one of the basic mechanisms that worked to unite and secure the family and the company. Derix shows that it is necessary to differentiate by gender here, but also by generation. The girls and young women were educated for generations in the institutions of the Sacré Cœur order, meaning they were firmly socialized by the schools to have Catholic values and into Catholic (elite) networks. The women bore the main responsibility for the continuation of the family's Catholic confinement. In the case of the boys, denominational ties ranked well behind the goal of education—defined in socioeconomic terms—as a way of preparing an for his professional life which unfolded within local, regional, national, and then increasingly international contexts. Consequently, a much stronger generational change can be observed among the young men: upper middle school and technical training for August Sr., *Realgymnasium* plus stays abroad and/or university studies for his sons, international secondary schools for the grandchildren.

Figure 1.4. Hans Heinrich Thyssen-Bornemisza ("Heini") with Margit ("Mama") and János ("Uncle János") Wettstein von Westersheimb, 26 July 1933, photographer unknown. Postcard from Scheveningen, postmark 27 July 1933.

Of course, this also meant that the sons were socialized into their parents' business-bourgeois networks, updating and expanding them, even if August Jr., for example, broke out of this mold. The military continued to serve as a source of socialization for August Sr. and his sons, where, privileged as so-called "one-year volunteers" ("Einjährig-Freiwillige"), they were required to serve only one year to earn the coveted reserve officer's commission. However, this no longer applied to the generation of the grandchildren. In stark terms, one might speak of a functional separation: girls were responsible for religion, boys for business.

By the end of her period of inquiry, Derix offers a whole new set of interpretations of the Thyssen family history. For all the Thyssens' susceptibility to conflict, she points to the astonishing longevity of their ties over decades, even across continents. Divorces admittedly meant the separation of a marriage, but "separations had a legal character with the Thyssens, and did not end the social relationship."[15] Derix could prove that divorced partners did not leave the family network but rather continuously expanded it after remarriage with their new families. Analogously, sibling relationships, however distant, proved to be "virtually impossible to sever." The family glue was its fortune, which not only had a powerful bonding effect but was handled differently by the generations. August Sr. and his children chose the path of mutual distancing and attempted exclusion, which was always painful and by no means always successful. For the generation of the grandchildren, however, it was different: although less central to Derix's study, they relied much more frequently on consensual, integrative measures. The period after 1945 accordingly marked a phase of transition for the Thyssens: of increased, now truly global mobility of their members; of the once again intensified transnational transfer of assets; and a certain consolidation of family relationships. Thus, as Gramlich's study of the art-collecting Thyssens describes, consensual strategies of decision-making can be observed above all in the Thyssen-Bornemisza line with Hans Heinrich and his siblings. This even included the willingness to satisfy the financial demands of other (ex-) family members away from the media spotlight, even though wealth always harbored further potential for conflict. The magnitude of the wealth, Derix concludes, correlates with its cohesive power in the family: "For the greater the pool of assets to be negotiated, the more it required resolution, the more likely disputes were, and the more it intensified familial interaction."

Lifestyle: Family Spaces, Local Roots, Mobility

After conflict, Simone Derix's study identifies the category of lifestyle (*Stil*) as a further axis of interpretation for exploring the history of the Thyssen family in the twentieth century. Broadly defined, it connotes a way of thinking and living, a value orientation, an emotional state, a kind of consumer behavior, and a mode of taste. This covers an expansive territory, which will be exemplified here by one central aspect: the production and use of familial spaces through the family's activities and their movements through space. A new path of analysis opens due to "both the spatial patterns of movement of the rich themselves, their specific modes of travel and the places they link with one another, along with the spatial mobility of their wealth."[16] Parallel to the further development of the group and the European and eventually worldwide expansion of the companies, the Thyssen network of family ties differentiated itself. It always had a local focus, albeit with different, sometimes several and changing geographical focal points. What these regional roots had in common, however, was that they always centered on the cultivation and staging of a specific lifestyle that was unique to the respective family member.

Associated with the individual lifestyle is a kind of retrospection that sheds a different light on the Thyssens' fierce disputes beyond the immediate cause of a conflict. In fact, Derix's study diagnoses a profound change in values, behavior, and consumption patterns that separated the generations of the family. More specifically, the company founder's ongoing crisis with his wife and children was a clash of diametrically opposed emotional needs, lifestyles, and ways of thinking. The findings suggest that the wide range of familial tensions is ultimately due to a significantly different way of dealing with wealth. As members of the ultra-wealthy who not only wanted to show their wealth to the outside world but also to enjoy it, the Thyssen children developed individual self-concepts and even self-dramatizations. This included conscious image cultivation, which found expression in the sense of Thorstein Veblen's "conspicuous consumption". While they distinguished themselves in highly individualized ways, this is precisely what expresses socially mediated behavior patterns of a privileged elite that demanded "individuality" from its members.[17] This transformation of ultra-wealthy lifestyles manifests itself in the conspicuous change in the use of space, including patterns of mobility.

Through the research of Jörg Lesczenski in particular, we already know a great deal about the daily life of August Thyssen Sr.[18] The rigid rhythm of his life, determined exclusively by the company, only varied on the days of his business trips, above all to the Ruhr and Rhineland regions, and to Berlin and the locations of Thyssen's ventures abroad. However, he always returned home.[19] In this sense, although August was professionally mobile and traveled a lot, he lived, as Derix notes, "monolocally" at only one residence. Residing in his first villa, which he moved into when he married in 1872, he was permanently anchored socially and regionally at Froschenteich in Mülheim-Styrum. The villa, which featured a park, fountain, stables, and two riding arenas, was in the immediate vicinity of a freight station, the company, and other commercial enterprises, which were as noisy as they were foul-smelling. He thus adhered for a very long time to the residential model of his childhood, in which family, acquisition, and social milieu spatially more or less fell into one.[20] It was only comparatively late in 1903—the Krupps' Villa Hügel had already been built between 1870 and 1873—and presumably under the influence of his socially ambitious children, that the now sixty-year-old August Thyssen bought Landsberg Castle near Kettwig in the vicinity of Essen with its surrounding extensive woodlands. Not only did he have it remodeled and decorated to suit the taste of the time,[21] but the property decoupled living and working. Its convenient location nevertheless combined the advantage of tranquility in a natural landscape with relative proximity to the businesses. Compared to other wealthy upper-class residences of the time, however, the isolated Landsberg Castle was peculiar to the Thyssen family. August Sr. bought it not least to reunite his squabbling family in situ and to secure his inheritance. There, he also received executives of his companies—something quite common in the Ruhr region, but not in the other economic regions of the Wilhelmine Empire. But the lord of the castle was ill-tempered and obstinate, his social networking with other industrialists was surprisingly limited, and he did not cultivate upper-class hospitality. It is fair to say that Landsberg Castle was characterized by "social ambiguity," which was also reflected in the architecture and aesthetics of the complex. It was here that old patterns of representation, such as the castle and the dynastic family residence, met the "new allegorical luxury" of the modern Art Nouveau bath, the acquired Rodin sculptures, and the tennis court.[22]

The person who came closest to his father's monolocality was Fritz, who was also rooted geographically in the Ruhr region. In this way, he demonstrated as the eldest son his claim to succession as company head. In 1897, during his military service in Düsseldorf, Fritz met Amélie Zurhelle, daughter of a prosperous but not affluent factory owner. Three years later, he married her against the wishes of his father and his brother August Jr. August Sr. sneered that Amélie was "pretty but trifling," that she only had "a sense for appearances." Her "extravagances" reminded him of his ex-wife's. He resorted to all manner of spiteful tactics to block the marriage but ultimately failed.[23] After the wedding, the couple first moved into the Oberhof, an old aristocratic residence owned by August Thyssen not far from the Gewerkschaft Deutscher Kaiser, where Fritz had served on the board since 1897. The eldest son thus maintained the close relationship between living and working that business owners in the nineteenth century, including his father, had cultivated. Fritz's intention to follow in his father's footsteps became even clearer when the couple took over August's villa at Froschenteich after the latter had moved to Landsberg Castle in 1904. The firstborn son's claim to succession gained visible expression.

Following the birth of their daughter Anita in May 1909, Fritz and Amélie had a reason to move to their own, now obviously very "large" house typical of a modern company boss, in a quiet forest setting. Following the family nomenclature, they built "Haus Thyssen," also known as "Villa Anita," in the Speldorfer Wald near Mülheim in the English country manor style with a surface area of 770 square meters and a bourgeois upper-class floor plan. The hall on the first floor and the dining room were more than eighty square meters in size. In contrast to August Sr., Fritz and Amélie used these spaces for the "grand" social occasions that were customary among the capitalist bourgeoisie. The villa was located on 70,000 square meters of land, increased to 150,000 square meters through acquisitions until the Nazis confiscated the property.[24]

By contrast, the ex-wife Hedwig and the other children behaved quite differently from August Sr. and Fritz. The second-born son August Jr. stands out.[25] Since 1897, he lived in conspicuous proximity to the emperor in Berlin. August Jr. chose the grand hotel as the form of habitation that fit his lifestyle. While he permanently occupied his suites, sometimes for years, he also always signaled by staying in a hotel an eventual change of location, the continuation of a journey. Grand hotels, a type of hotel that had become established since the founding of the empire, were the place for an urban, highly mobile, and dizzyingly wealthy upper class of aristocracy and business-oriented bourgeoisie. In Habbo Knoch's words, they were hubs for the "circulation of power, capital, and status."[26]

Of course, August Sr. and Fritz also stayed in splendid hotels during their visits to Berlin, preferably in the Continental at the Friedrichstraße station, which opened in 1885 with its more than two hundred rooms. Equipped for guests of conservative taste, it was frequented by the provincial and military aristocracy. August Jr., on the other hand, first lodged in the fashionable Monopol, which counted among its attractions a "Moorish" café. Later, he stayed in the Bristol on Unter den Linden, which advertised with the slogans like "The most international. The greatest social destination. . . . Pre-eminently American and English."[27] August Jr. later moved to the Esplanade on Potsdamer Platz, opened in 1908, with a glass-domed conservatory as a lounge area for sophisticated conviviality in the English style. Between 1926 and 1936, the great first-class hotels in Paris (the Claridge on the Champs-Élysées and the Royal Monceau on the Avénue Hoche) were August Jr.'s fashionable ports of call.

The grand hotels offered their guests a novel blend of public and private life that was particularly well-suited to the ultra-wealthy lifestyle. The first floor, with its accessible dining and conference halls, reading rooms, conservatories, stores, and smoking and music salons, represented a semi-public space for socializing that became the interface of early high society in European metropolises. As Derix could show, that is precisely why the opulent big-city hotels were so appealing to August Jr. He was not only concerned with being "very rich," after all, but first and foremost with being "in." In the semi-private rooms of the grand hotels, accessible to the boulevard press, the aristocracy and the upper-class elite met the nouveau riche, social climbers met the jeunesse dorée, and swindlers mingled with stars and starlets. Even though he had gone bankrupt with his own cement works, August Jr. was able to finance his steady residence by means of his father's continued generous allowance, by taking on debt, and through the credit that the grand hotels granted him on a permanent basis because of the Thyssen name. Part of the family's wealth was thus the pedigree, which signaled creditworthiness. August Jr.'s signature was even recognized as a means of payment in certain Berlin circles. But the scandal-prone August Jr. should not be underestimated. Derix shows that he represented a Thyssen "outpost in Paris,"[28] performing valuable "relationship building"[29] for himself and his brothers Fritz and Heinrich. He managed to gain access to the leading political and economic circles in France, which is also to say, he invested his accumulated social capital specifically in the interests of increasing the wealth of all Thys-

Figure 1.5. The Grandhotel as a social hub. The extended Thyssen family network at the Dunapalota Hotel (Danube Palace) in Budapest, September 1939 (from left: Adèle Bornemisza, Margit and János Wettstein von Westersheimb, Gabrielle and Adolph Bentinck van Schoonheten). Written postcard. Photographer unknown.

sen siblings. Thus, August Jr.'s role fits in with observations made at the same time for the internationally expanding family networks of private bankers: "Often, it was especially the second- or third-born male offspring who expanded the family resource pool by ensuring the establishment of a foreign contact and kinship network."[30]

Heinrich Thyssen, for his part, pursued a remarkably inter- and transnational lifestyle,[31] which was intended to ensure one thing above all: maximum spatial distance to the patriarch on the Ruhr through "purposefully distancing" himself.[32] After an interlude in London high society, he transformed himself into a Hungarian aristocrat by marrying the baroness Margit from the old Hungarian noble family of Bornemisza in June 1906, dressed in Hungarian magnate's costume at the Schottenkirche in Vienna. Heinrich secured access to this aristocratic elite through his fortune and marriage, but then had to perform further public "integration efforts" in order to belong "properly" and permanently. He thus took Hungarian citizenship and then had himself adopted by his father-in-law Gábor, who had neither money nor a male heir (but three daughters). In legal terms, from then on, Heinrich had two living fathers. In June 1907 Emperor Franz Joseph awarded him the hereditary title of "Baron Thyssen-Bornemisza de Kászon." The trade-off of

Figure 1.6. Heinrich Thyssen-Bornemisza (r.) in Hungarian magnate costume (*díszmagyar*). On the left, probably his father-in-law and adoptive father Gábor Baron Bornemisza de Kászon in the uniform of a first lieutenant (*főhadnagy*) of the Szeged Landwehr Hussar Regiment No. 3, ca. 1910. Photographer unknown.

this "deal" was that Heinrich paid his parents-in-law and adoptive parents a generous lifelong allowance.

In the very year of his marriage, Heinrich acquired the requisite trappings of a Hungarian magnate, namely the Rohoncz (Rechnitz) estate with its castle, manor, and hunting grounds, which allowed him to develop a corresponding lifestyle.[33] The castle, which no longer exists, had more than 220 rooms and encompassed an estate of more than 2,000 hectares. As Derix demonstrates, Heinrich transformed the estate into "our castle," the ancestral seat of the Thyssen-Bornemiszas.[34] The property's dimensions clearly put the father in his place symbolically in his home Ruhr region: Heinrich's manor dwarfed Landsberg Castle. Competition and conflict between the Thyssens were also played out for all to see at the level of the size and furnishings of their respective homes.

With the demise of the Danube monarchy, Heinrich's living and mobility patterns changed. At the end of March 1919, the family and their three children fled the bloody fighting resulting from the Hungarian soviet republic and never returned, even though their property was in fact restored to them. They made their way to the Netherlands, which had been neutral during the world war and fulfilled a central economic function for the deeply riven postwar Europe, but also for Thyssen's ventures. After a stopover in the fashionable seaside resort of Scheveningen, the Thyssen-Bornemiszas moved to The Hague. From 1921 at the latest, they lived in a representative villa on the edge of the Statenkwartier, one of the most exalted residential areas.[35]

Heinrich had been increasingly engaged in various tasks within the family-owned companies since 1913. When he moved to the Netherlands, he joined the Bank voor Handel en Scheepvaart, the international financial hub of Thyssen's ventures in Rotterdam. But Heinrich characteristically chose as his residence the seat of the royal court and government. The city touted itself as an international financial and service epicenter, as well as a booming haven for the rich and super-rich, playing host to twenty-five of the country's top one hundred taxpayers. An international clientele of politicians and diplomats had also settled there since the Hague Conferences of 1899 and 1907. The urban society was less national and bourgeois than international and highly affluent, which was exactly what the Thyssen-Bornemiszas were looking for.

After his separation (1928) and later divorce (1932) from his first wife Margit, Heinrich traveled widely. He gradually embraced the lifestyle of his brother August and discovered the world of grand hotels for himself, which were also always sites for matchmaking. According to Simone Derix, they made it seem as if the ultra-rich were "always in the right company." Heinrich would meet his future wives here: Maud Feller, a much sought-after photographic model, and Gunhild von Fabrice, a fashion model, were both members of the jet set.[36]

After the Netherlands, Switzerland increasingly established itself as an international financial center. Heinrich followed the trend. Hand in hand with Swiss citizenship and negotiated tax advantages, he acquired the huge Villa Favorita on Lake Lugano from a Prussian prince in 1932.[37] More than just the dimensions of the Favorita recall the Rohoncz (Rechnitz) family estate. The villa in Lugano-Castagnola at the foot of Monte Brè was to house Heinrich's valuable art collection, which had been transferred to the Rohoncz Castle Art Collection Foundation the year before to prevent the art assets from being divided up. Within its estate of over forty thousand square meters, the Favorita also included the Casa rossa (kitchen and living quarters of the servants) and four other smaller villas, which were used to accommodate guests or to store valuables and commodities. This is where Heinrich withdrew from the public eye, becoming virtually "invisible" to the media behind the walls of the Favorita. Even if the sources do not permit a complete reconstruction, much evidence suggests that while Heinrich outwardly resided monolocally in Lugano, he was de facto highly mobile. He continually traveled across Europe to places that gave him access to the international affluent circles. As an example, Simone Derix recreated from the files Heinrich's itinerary for 1937: In a little over six months, from early April to mid-November, he made overseas stops in seventeen locations in nine states, some multiple times.[38] In other words, Heinrich Thyssen-Bornemisza also spent much of his life on the move, traveling throughout Europe and spending his days in hotel suites.

But even Fritz, who was supposedly so "German" and demonstratively rooted in the Ruhr region, was constantly traveling, alone or with his wife Amélie, and thus corresponded to the period's highly mobile lifestyle of the ultra-rich.[39] They demonstrated through their travels that they had several houses, apartments, and hotel suites in various places, i.e., sufficient wealth to be able to afford such a lifestyle, which included expensive habits such as spa treatments, dinners, balls, and evening parties. By the same token, it was the social stability of the locales that socially anchored and facilitated the mobile lifestyles of the well-to-do: "Hotels, restaurants, and clubs functioned as a nerve center where the ultra-rich could predictably meet other wealthy people."[40]

The Thyssens' busy travels followed seasonal as well as geographic patterns, reproducing the previously mentioned intergenerational differences. August Sr. had himself traveled privately, which had become customary from the 1830s as part of an affluent lifestyle. The company founder's destination was the genteel spa and bathing resorts in Germany and Austria (Oberstdorf, Wiesbaden, Baden-Baden, Bad Gastein),[41] the motivation for the trips was to preserve or restore health. In keeping with the medical knowledge of the time, he maintained complete rest and inactivity, such as lying down in open air on the balcony, supplemented by cold and hot rubs.[42]

Although he suffered from a heart condition, Heinrich seems to have deliberately avoided his father's spa resorts.[43] The Thyssen siblings' itineraries took them to other European countries, with Heinrich going to Merano or Capri at an early age.[44] They preferred to go to the Italian and French Rivieras, where the seasonal rhythms were also different. Thus, if one traveled to the German spas during the summer season, the Riviera provided the ideal destination for the winter months. Due to tabloid coverage, the socially exclusive character of places like Cannes, Nice, Monte Carlo, or San Remo was legend. The Majestic in Cannes, for example, built entirely in Art Nouveau style, became August Jr.'s favorite vacation retreat. There, he wove his network of contacts in France. His itineraries attest to his skill at adapting to the preferred locations of the French elites: in winter on the Côte d'Azur, in the summer months on the northern Atlantic in Deauville, which combined the advantages of the fashionable seaside resort with marina and casino and the mecca of French horse racing, where "one" would spend the racing season.[45] In addition, the sophisticated, internationally frequented Carlsbad, with its grand hotels and casinos, attracted members of European royal families, aristocrats and higher statesmen alike from the mid-nineteenth century onward and, and besides drinking cures, relied above all on the socially therapeutic effect of the visiting social elite. Heinrich came here with his family, but Fritz also visited Carlsbad several times in the summer,[46] though, more like his father than the brothers, mainly for preventative healthcare. Indeed, for such stays, sporting and social reasons had long since taken precedence over medicinal therapy. Southern sun, blue sea, and warm temperatures came into vogue. As the siblings Erika and Klaus Mann put it in 1931: "You don't even have to be sick" to go to the Riviera. They relished the fact that nothing more was expected of them beyond "a very little bit of golf or tennis."[47]

Both brothers, Fritz and Heinrich, also indulged in the popular fad among the super-rich to travel to Egypt in the winter for recreation. Thus, as early as March 1906, we find Fritz and Amélie in the venerable Shepheard's Hotel in Cairo, built in 1841 and expanded five times. It was the starting point for cruises on the Nile, for which Thomas Cook had enjoyed a monopoly since 1880.[48] In 1908, the couple's long-distance trips became more frequent: India and Ceylon, then a round trip of several weeks from Budapest to Odessa, Constantinople, Belgrade, and back. In the winter of 1927/28 Fritz and Amélie traveled again to Egypt, as did Heinrich, who was so enthusiastic about it that he planned a Nile tour for the following year together with his brother August. Heinrich also spent several winters in Egypt in the 1930s, where he was accompanied by various family members.[49]

Figure 1.7. Fritz and Amélie Thyssen in Carlsbad, 1907. Photographer unknown.

Figure 1.8. Heinrich and Margit Thyssen-Bornemisza with their son Stephan, Carlsbad, August 1917. Photographer unknown.

Increasingly, however, St. Moritz in Switzerland was becoming a magnet for the Thyssens in the winter. The boom of secluded, palatial mountain hotels in hitherto undeveloped mountain regions had begun in the 1880s.[50] Already before World War I, August Sr.'s brother Joseph discovered Engadin for the family. Later, almost all the Thyssens would find their way there, especially August Jr., Heinrich, and Maud, and, in the 1950s, Hans Heinrich. This was due in no small part to the rise of winter sports, which were intensively pursued by body-conscious family members such as Maud Feller, who, as a member of high society, attached great importance to sports and body sculpting in her everyday life.

It may be observed that all of August Thyssen's sons were highly mobile and moved around Europe and the world with great ease and regularity, following the seasonal trends and local preferences of the ultra-rich. In Derix's words, they led "a privileged, multi-residential nomadic life."[51] As a family, the Thyssens created inter- and transnational fields of action through their global encounters. This also applies to Fritz Thyssen and his wife, despite their growing nationalist and politically conservative orientation.

"Calculated Risk": The Thyssens, Their Foundations and Advisors

Under the heading of "Calculated Risk," Simone Derix's study summarizes a series of family strategies for protecting Thyssen's fortune, as it was broadly defined by the research network.[52] Fritz and Heinrich Thyssen, to whom substantial parts of the group passed in the 1920s, managed to separate their shares in the company through several exchange and sales maneuvers. With this phrase, she highlights the fact that while, The various branches of the family, however, as Derix highlights, nonetheless remained intertwined until the second half of the twentieth century through foundations and other "financial structures" (companies, trusts, and holdings). After all, at the turn of the century already, the Thyssen group was no longer purely "German" but transnationally networked. Nor was it the creation of a few prominent male company founders, but a family project. Along similar lines, Ingo Köhler discovered cross-border "networked wealth" for the same period among private bankers. They, too, materially increased and simultaneously socially stabilized their wealth "by means of network-bound processes."[53]

Despite all the conflict, the unifying bond of the entire family was to protect this "network of assets" bearing the Thyssen name—against war, revolution, and state intervention, but also against destructive behavior from within the family—using a variety of strategies. The focus was on the global diversification of capital, i.e., the internationalization of assets through various wealth transfer strategies. This, in turn, made the group of financial and legal advisors mentioned above pivotal—it was in their hands that "the financial fortunes of the family members largely rested."54 Over the decades, the Thyssens nurtured an almost family-specific advising culture.

It is not the purpose here, however, to trace the geographic expansion of Thyssen's ventures even before World War I, whether through concessions (Russia, North Africa, India, Norway), through the purchase of ore fields (Lorraine, Normandy), or through a broad network of trading organizations (Netherlands, France, Italy, North Africa, Argentina). This international economic expansion increasingly collided with the intensifying political nationalization during and after World War I, which provoked family camouflaging strategies of acquiring, depositing, and protecting wealth without explicit connection to the "Thyssen" name. In concluding her study, Derix points out that people in transnational relational webs create "their own cartography of the world," in which states that are not usually the focus of disciplines like international relations or international history become prominent in a striking way.55

In this connection, the family gained room to maneuver in the 1920s primarily in the Netherlands, later in Switzerland. Harald Wixforth and Boris Gehlen took up on this thread within the scope of the research network. They centered on the previously little-known corporate complex of the Thyssen-Bornemisza line and illuminated it from a corporate-historical perspective.56 Due to its wartime neutrality, the stability of its currency (the guilder was pegged to gold!), and the strict maintenance of banking secrecy to protect it from outside interference,57 the Netherlands became the first international financial hub for wealthy individuals from the losing countries of the world war. They had been denied access to the financial centers of the Allies for a period of five years after the armistice. The Thyssen companies, which were dependent on imports of raw materials and therefore on foreign currency, had been active in Rotterdam since 1918 with the Bank voor Handel en Scheepvaart (BHS),58 whose management Heinrich took over a year later. Other trading and asset management companies, closely intertwined through mutual holdings, soon followed; they administered several family foundations, most of which, however, were then domiciled in Switzerland. This created a veritable "network of assets." The entire Thyssen family used their Dutch foundations as an outwardly disguised "repository for the financial capital of the companies as well as for their private funds."59 They also conducted their financial transactions through them: August Sr. still focused primarily on the manufacturing businesses; Heinrich, August Jr., and Fritz as well as their cousins Hans and Julius from the Joseph Thyssen line focused chiefly on controlling and protecting their wealth. The Thyssens were also involved from the outset in the new financial center of New York, which was emerging after World War I. They founded the Union Banking Corporation (UBC) in August 1924, which handled financial transactions with the

Dutch institutions until the 1940s. On the outside, US bankers acted like the Harriman brothers, so that the bank's ties to the Thyssen family remained completely hidden.

In the Thyssen asset network, Switzerland, as mentioned above, was the seat of several foundations the family set up in the 1920s as new means of wealth protection. The neutral country presented the advantage of permitting wealth to be deposited securely. To date, however, research has mainly dealt with charitable foundations and has almost completely ignored family foundations. This has also meant overlooking their international, cross-border mode of operation, which was made all the easier by the fact that foundations are set up to act discreetly and generally do not leave behind any public records. Only the American historian David Sabean, taking the example of the Siemens family in the nineteenth century, has interpreted foundations as institutions that help ultra-rich families create internal cohesion. For the Thyssens, questions of asset management and organization only became a priority when August Sr. divided up his company *inter vivos* to his sons Fritz and Heinrich since1919/21.[60] This sparked a series of further divisions, exchanges, and reallocations of shareholdings after his death in 1926.

Simone Derix sheds light on numerous Thyssen family foundations that were previously unknown. Under Swiss law, family foundations did not have to be made public, so only insiders knew the true connections. In addition, the country lured people with very low tax rates. Thus, on 18 December 1926, Dutch plenipotentiaries established the Kaszony Family Foundation in the town of Schwyz for Heinrich Thyssen-Bornemisza. The name of the foundation alluded to his Hungarian title of nobility without naming him. The foundation board consisted exclusively of Heinrich himself, who was also the sole foundation beneficiary. As per its unambiguous purpose, the foundation acted as a holding company for Heinrich's assets, over which he alone had the right to dispose. But the foundation structure meant that the assets now belonged to a Swiss legal entity managed from the Netherlands. The transferred assets were now practically untouchable, since the foundation detached them from the person of the founder and secured them against any kind of seizure, both state and family. Heinrich's aim was to protect his assets, be it after his death or as a result of a divorce, from being divided up through systematic internationalization. He pursued the same purpose with the Rohoncz Castle Art Collection Foundation (here, too, the allusion was to Hungary), presumably also established in 1926. Heinrich transferred to it his art collection, and later the entire Villa Favorita complex: All kinds of assets—money, shareholdings, funds, real estate, art—were to be held together and protected from division by a transnational, completely opaque web of assets, which in turn was also linked to the producing enterprises through shareholdings.

Fritz Thyssen followed the same path of protecting his assets from internal and external access, with the difference being that he did not act as founder himself but instead appointed his mother Hedwig, who in the meantime had Belgian citizenship. In 1931, with the aid of some of the same agents from the Netherlands that had helped initiate the Kaszony Foundation, Hedwig then established the Pelzer Foundation in the canton of Glarus, bearing her maiden name. Hedwig was the founder, the sole beneficiary of the foundation, and, at least initially, the only member of the foundation board. The Pelzer Foundation was also run from the Netherlands. Its purpose was to "support family members and preserve inherited family assets." The Pelzer Foundation was, as Derix reveals, Fritz Thyssen's response to the German Reich's foreign exchange controls. These were introduced in August/October 1931 in the wake of the world economic crisis in order to control all foreign exchange transactions.

German citizens were legally obliged to declare their assets abroad to the Reichsbank. Fritz used the capital transfers to the Pelzer Foundation to dispose of his foreign assets to an external third party. As a result, he could conceal them from German tax authorities and avoid paying taxes. With the help of the foundation, however, Fritz was also able to surreptitiously carry out financial transactions and acquire new assets without drawing attention to himself. His acquisition of eleven hundred gold bars, which were stored in London, is notorious. It was not until World War II, starting in 1940, when the Nazis occupied the Netherlands, that the Pelzer Foundation was exposed as the perfect "smokescreen" for many years. It re-emerged when the Allies dealt with the confiscation of enemy assets and, after the war, when they were confronted with Fritz's restitution claims. Jan Schleusener's research into the expropriation of Fritz Thyssen's assets has reconstructed in detail the investigations of the German tax and foreign exchange authorities before and after 1939, as well as those of the British agents.[61]

Though not in the form of foundations, other entities were set up in Switzerland, the United States, and Argentina for the purpose of securing and increasing wealth in a "cross-border interplay of wealthy individuals, banks, financial and legal advisors" that was hidden from the view of national governments.[62] With the help of Faminta AG, founded in the canton of Glarus as a joint stock corporation in February 1929, Fritz Thyssen took out foreign loans for his German companies, but he also secured their foreign assets against possible confiscation. He also used it after the outbreak of the war to protect private family wealth. The Overseas Trust, founded in September/October 1939 in Vaduz in Liechtenstein, served the welfare and financial security of Fritz's daughter Anita, now married Zichy. Moreover, Colamina S.A. in Buenos Aires, established in 1938, acted as a holding company to manage and increase the assets acquired in Argentina.

It is abundantly clear at this point that the advisors and experts described above as integral to the Thyssen family and business history (e.g., financial advisors, consultants, lawyers/legal experts, executors) were immensely important for the global diversification of assets. They were an essential part of Thyssen's international wealth network as "financial architects and representatives" ("Konstrukteure und Mandatsträger"). Despite the very patchy nature of the sources, the research project made it possible for the first time to wrest them from their anonymity and identify them as discreet but all-the-more powerful actors. In their dual function, they had not only the ability to give advice but also the power to act—for the companies; in the administration of property and estates, legal proceedings, and tax and nationality issues; and as mediators in the numerous family conflicts (inheritance disputes, divorces, allowances, and disbursements). Had it been advertised, their job profile would have been both broad and demanding. Required were "expertise, creativity, a willingness to communicate as well as discretion, and a high degree of individual commitment that extended from a change of residence to a change of nationality. According to Derix, they "combined advice with action, reflection on structures with the power to shape them."[63] For the family, though, this also entailed the danger of a loss of control and growing dependency in its increasingly unmanageable, intricately interwoven financial relationships.

The project used the quantitative method of social network analysis to identify those advisors to the Thyssens in the first half of the twentieth century who held key importance as "nodes" in the family's wide-ranging wealth network. While more than one hundred were recorded, Derix characterizes twelve as "advisors in a meta-position." Over a long period, they either worked across borders and issues or were responsible for specific countries and areas of responsibility. Most importantly, they decided whether other experts should be consulted and, if so, which ones: "They oversaw the accumulated knowledge. They filtered it for their clients."[64] While forming a thoroughly heterogeneous group, they nonetheless shared one distinguishing factor: with few exceptions, they held a position at some point in their careers at one of the three Thyssen banks—BHS, UBC, and August-Thyssen-Bank (ATB).

Using network analysis,[65] Derix identifies, for example, those men who frequently occupied an intermediary position between other nodes in the network and thus had powerful opportunities for monitoring and control ("betweenness centrality"). She further pinpoints those men who were close to central decision-makers. The same names invariably emerge: the Swiss banker Heinrich Blass, for example, a leading figure at Crédit Suisse in the 1930s; Johann Georg Gröninger, Edward Roland Harriman, August Thyssen's trusted lawyer Carl Härle, Fritz Jacke, Cornelis Lievense, Wilhelm Roelen, Robert van Aken, and above all Hendrik Jozef Kouwenhoven. Härle and

Jacke had already earned the trust of the family during the heated family feuds before World War I. They subsequently rose to leading positions in various Thyssen companies and rendered valuable services in managing and safeguarding the family's wealth.

Kouwenhoven, for his part, was involved in the financial affairs of both brothers as the pivotal figure of the BHS. He might be described as their go-between. He was also responsible for negotiating the financial well-being of August Jr., his sister Hedwig, and the grandchildren. He was virtually omnipresent in Thyssen's global wealth network. In the Netherlands, but also in Germany, he held prominent positions in companies, banks, and foundations. Derix manages to create a concise short portrait of the previously little-known, pious Kouwenhoven, of reformed Protestant denomination, father of fifteen children, who, according to contemporary witnesses, had remarkable negotiating skills. Nonetheless, he was relieved of his duties by Heinrich in the early 1940s for using his authority against the interests of the Thyssen-Bornemiszas.[66]

In this context, the end of World War II was a profound turning point not only politically but also in terms of family history. A generational change took place in several respects: not only did Heinrich Thyssen-Bornemisza (1947) and Fritz Thyssen (1951) die—August Jr. had already passed away in 1943—but so did five of their most important advisers, including the three (Jacke, Härle, Kouwenhoven) who had held the reins of the family's finances since 1918/19. The baton was passed to August's grandchildren, who faced the challenge of having to figure out the interwoven financial web for themselves. The group of experts advising them had to be reconfigured. Men like Robert Ellscheid, Robert Pferdmenges, Kurt Birrenbach, and Hans-Günther Sohl moved to the front of the Fritz Thyssen family line. This marked a new beginning in many respects, not just in terms of personnel. Within the project, the studies by Johannes Bähr and Hans Günter Hockerts explore against the backdrop of the early Federal Republic the reconfiguration of the network of advisors around Amélie Thyssen with its notable proximity to Konrad Adenauer. Boris Gehlen did the same for the Thyssen-Bornemiszas.

In retrospect, however, a further aspect becomes clear. Namely, the nation-state and an international order based on national sovereignty remained potent in the twentieth century, as evidenced by the confiscation of enemy assets in wartime and seizures for political reasons. But nation states met their limits when it came to the unambiguous national classification of people and assets. While their power ended at national borders, wealth enjoyed the advantage of being able to cross them. In this respect, the Thyssens offer an opportunity to research into a heretofore missing "history of wealth infrastructures."[67]

Figure 1.9. The network of advisors around Amélie Thyssen, 17 March 1967: Kurt Birrenbach, Robert Ellscheid, Hans-Günther Sohl. Photo: Works photographer at August Thyssen-Hütte AG.

Notes

1. Derix, *Die Thyssens*, 38–46.
2. A little over a year after the end of World War II, many members of the Thyssen family were unable to travel to Switzerland for the wedding. Fritz was interned, Heinrich was absent due to illness. Even if they were absent, the Thyssen(-Bornemisza)s nevertheless formed the center of a socially far-reaching, aristocratic family network. The Bornemisza, Batthyány, Bentinck van Schoonheten, Wettstein von Westersheimb, Lippe-Weißenfeld (father of the bride), and Schönborn-Buchheim (mother of the bride) families were represented at the wedding. The "family cardinal" August Heimbach, a great-nephew of August Thyssen, embodies the Thyssens' traditional attachment to Catholicism.

3. Derix, "Grenzenloses Vermögen," 179; in detail on the employees, Derix, *Die Thyssens*, 216–32. Two examples may be mentioned: After the divorce of August and Hedwig Thyssen, the governess Minna Schlömann took the place of the mother for the four small children. Heinrich and Margit Thyssen-Bornemisza separated at the end of the 1920s and left the house they shared in The Hague, where their youngest son Hans Heinrich was left alone to grow up in a permanent circle of trusted domestic servants until he graduated from high school in 1939.
4. See also Schäfer, *Familienunternehmen*, 226.
5. This is discussed in detail in Derix, "Transnationale Familien."
6. Review by Christopher Kopper, in *Historische Zeitschrift* 305 (2017): 599f.
7. Köhler, "Vernetzter Reichtum," 63f.
8. Gajek and Kurr, "Reichtum," 9–31 (quotes 15, 28).
9. Cf., e.g., Lesczenski, *August Thyssen*, 76, 79f., 86, 117f.
10. Lesczenski, "Aufstieg," 83.
11. Cf. in detail Koch, "Inhaber der elterlichen Sorge," 1210–15.
12. Nipperdey, *Arbeitswelt*, 99.
13. Cf. August Thyssen's letters to Carl Klönne of July and August 1902, quoted in Lesczenski, *August Thyssen*, 123.
14. Hockerts, *Erbe*, 93, 298.
15. The following quotes to the end of the paragraph from Derix, *Die Thyssens*, 472f.
16. Derix, "Grenzenloses Vermögen," 164.
17. Cf. also Willems, "Individualität," 177, 198f., albeit in a different historical context.
18. Cf. Lesczenski, *August Thyssen*; for a concise history of August Thyssen's life up to World War I, see Lesczenski, "Aufstieg."
19. For an example of a reconstructed itinerary, see Lesczenski, *August Thyssen*, 101.
20. Cf. Derix, *Die Thyssens*, 108, 110, 112f.
21. Cf. in detail the weighty volume by Hassler, Nußbaum, and Plumpe, *Unternehmer*, containing numerous illustrations and essays on the purchase, planning, reconstruction, and furnishing of Landsberg Castle in historical comparison.
22. Ibid, 11f.; in comparison with the sociability and lifestyle of other upper-middle-class families, Wörner and Lesczenski, "Geselligkeiten," esp. 478–81.
23. Lesczenski, *August Thyssen*, 119f.; Eglau, *Fritz Thyssen*, 31–35; August Thyssen to Carl Klönne, 11 July 1902, quoted in ibid. 34.
24. Derix, *Die Thyssens*, 113–23; Gramlich, *Kunstsammler*, 118.
25. Unless otherwise stated, the following is taken from Derix, *Die Thyssens*, 123–40.
26. Knoch, *Grandhotels*, esp. 15–20 (quote 23), also 21, 26.
27. Berlin und die Berliner: Leute, Dinge, Sitten, Winke (Karlsruhe, 1905), quoted in Derix, *Die Thyssens*, 126; see also Knoch, *Grandhotels*, 171f., 193, 295, 301, 318, 348.
28. For more details on August Jr., see Derix, *Die Thyssens*, 134–40 (quote 134).
29. Bourdieu, "Mechanismen," 67.
30. Köhler, "Vernetzter Reichtum," 67.
31. Unless otherwise stated, the following is taken from Derix, *Die Thyssens*, 140–61.
32. For more details, see Derix, "Familiale Distanzen."
33. Illustrations in Rasch, *Briefe*, 38, 97.
34. Cf. photographs ibid., 70, and Derix, *Die Thyssens*, 148f. (quote 149).
35. There are no photographs or descriptions of the interior of the Thyssen-Bornemiszas' townhouse at Stadhouderslaan 126. For this and the following, see ibid., 154–61.

36. Ibid., 212. On Maud Feller's life in detail, ibid., 130–34; on the "mobility and matchmaking" of the Thyssens, ibid., 212–16.
37. Hereafter, according to ibid., 162–73.
38. Cf. ibid., 206, Heinrich's movement pattern from 1937. In addition to the most frequented track between Lugano and Berlin, the following visited sites are noteworthy: Venice, Lucerne, Basel, Paris, Brussels, London, The Hague, Münster, Heidelberg, Baden-Baden, Munich, Hamburg, Carlsbad, Vienna, and Rechnitz.
39. Cf. ibid., 116–23.
40. Derix, "Grenzenloses Vermögen," 173.
41. Cf. August's letters in Rasch, *Briefe*, 113, 115, 117, 123, 126–28, 146, 326, 359–67, 378.
42. Ibid., 128: August Thyssen to Heinrich Thyssen-Bornemisza, 12 February 1920.
43. Unless otherwise stated, the following is taken from Derix, *Die Thyssens*, 195–212.
44. Cf. for 1922, e.g., Rasch, *Briefe*, 147, 153.
45. For August Jr., stays in Cannes in 1927 and 1928 and in Deauville and Vichy for 1927 are reliably documented. Although the sources are extremely fragmentary, they suggest that he regularly visited spas and seaside resorts. Cf. Derix, *Die Thyssens*, 203.
46. Heinrich Thyssen-Bornemisza's summer stays in Carlsbad can be traced for the years 1905, 1917, 1923–26, 1928 and 1929, 1932–34, 1937, and 1938; Fritz Thyssen's for the years 1907, 1909, 1928, 1931, and 1932.
47. Erika Mann/Klaus Mann, *Das Buch von der Riviera* (1931), quoted in Derix, *Die Thyssens*, 201.
48. See esp. Knoch, *Grandhotels*, 142.
49. Heinrich's stays in Egypt in the winters of 1936/37, 1937/38, and 1938/39 are documented. On the Egyptian tours of both brothers, see Derix, *Die Thyssens*, 209–12.
50. See also Knoch, *Grandhotels*, 141.
51. Derix, "Grenzenloses Vermögen," 178.
52. Unless otherwise stated, the following is taken from Derix, *Die Thyssens*, 323–412.
53. Köhler, "Vernetzter Reichtum," 60, 72 (quote 60).
54. Derix, *Die Thyssens*, 323f. (quote 324).
55. Ibid, 475.
56. Wixforth, *Stahlkonzern*, 65–113; Gehlen, *Thyssen-Bornemisza-Gruppe*, esp. 17–19, 176–81, 332–68.
57. For the Dr. Oetker family of entrepreneurs, see Finger, "Reiche Lebenswelten," esp. 88f.
58. See also Gehlen, *Thyssen-Bornemisza-Gruppe*, 29f., 36–38.
59. Derix, *Die Thyssens*, 337 (quote). The various Thyssen foundations in the Netherlands and Switzerland could only be painstakingly reconstructed after the end World War II by the British and American authorities during confiscations of enemy assets and subsequent restitutions.
60. A smaller part went to their cousins Hans and Julius from the Joseph Thyssen line of the family.
61. Schleusener, *Enteignung*, esp. 113–34.
62. Derix, *Die Thyssens*, 360.
63. Ibid., 362f.
64. Ibid., 365.
65. Ibid., 366–68.
66. For details on Kouwenhoven's dismissal, see also Gehlen, *Thyssen-Bornemisza-Gruppe*, 59–68.
67. Derix, *Die Thyssens*, 474f.

CHAPTER 2

TWO CIVIC LIVES IN THE PUBLIC EYE
The Brothers Fritz Thyssen and Heinrich Thyssen-Bornemisza

(Felix de Taillez, 2017)

Felix de Taillez focuses on the brothers Fritz Thyssen and Heinrich Thyssen (-Bornemisza), the well-known sons of the company's founder, in the context of media history. Historical research on wealth now recognizes the central importance of mediated (self-)representations of the rich and super-rich. This applies to both the genesis of the modern public sphere via the mass media and to the constitution of the group of the super-rich, which itself is socially quite differentiated. Media visibility increasingly became a possible means of social positioning.[1] Fritz and Heinrich in fact appear almost as counterfigures in the media: Fritz operated openly in the political limelight from 1923 at the latest, when he achieved national fame through his resistance against the French occupiers. He became publicly visible through the media, sometimes spectacularly. This contrasts with Heinrich's limited media presence: at first glance, he was apolitical and surfaced in the mass media only two or three times. Nevertheless, he was visible in exclusive public spheres such as the Austro-Hungarian aristocracy, the art collector scene, and the horse-breeding and horse-racing community, each with its own very limited target audience and distinctive media.

Derix's study already showed that while the brothers led different lifestyles and went their own ways in business, they were alike in their strategies for securing and increasing their assets and remained closely linked in the Thyssen wealth network. Felix de Taillez also looks for commonalities beyond the observation that the brothers were the subject, like all intrafamily disputes of the Thyssens in general, of a lively media interest in the daily and tabloid press. In this regard, they were also always medially constructed figures to whom "typical" characteristics and behaviors were attributed.

But de Taillez's focus goes beyond the level of media attributions. It tackles the brothers' experience with the media as well as their own media-related activities. The Thyssens had a tradition of using modern media for their own ends. After all, going back to August Sr., the family had made aggressive use of the media resources available at the time: in advertising for their companies, but also in publicly airing private disputes. De Taillez traces the brothers' media strategies—one might even say media policies—including the creation and cultivation of a personal image. He defines his historical period of investigation as the "mass media *Sattelzeit*" (according to Reinhart Koselleck; literally: 'saddle period') when modern communication media profoundly transformed politics and society and created a new kind of "media culture" that necessitated contemporaries become media conscious. He thereby also systematically examines the other side of media presence: the deliberate avoidance of publicity, the "invisible" activities in personal networks and in the no less powerful backrooms of politics and society. Accordingly, the study is framed in terms of the guiding thesis "that the behaviors of the two brothers were molded by distinctive media experiences. They both, in their own ways, sought to use them to further their different political, social, business, or cultural ambitions."[2]

De Taillez is thus not concerned with writing a dual biography. Indeed, as Heinrich is considerably more difficult to grasp as a person than his brother Fritz in the available sources, the portrayal is necessarily asymmetrical. The narrative of Fritz and Heinrich rather reflects the medial nature of the brothers' story. Here, de Taillez, who researched in forty archives and evaluated more than 150 print media and news agencies, takes as his starting point a broadly defined concept of media: Not only are the usual mass media studied as media, but the body, clothing, the architecture of buildings, etc., also have medial qualities and are analyzed as such. Reviews in this context were interested not only in the development of the German as well as international news market relevant to media history but also and especially in the significance of individual media practices for corporate strategic interests and decision-making.[3]

Stepping Out of the Father's Shadow: Fritz Thyssen as National Hero

Shortly after World War I, Fritz discovered national politics as a platform for making his own mark in contrast to his father and for establishing his identity as more than just the "son of August Thyssen."[4] His father had not so much been regionally as locally visible: as honorary citizen of Hamborn, patron of the arts, and benefactor. In contrast, his firstborn scaled the ladder of media attention in the first half of the 1920s as a national political hero. He thus publicly detached himself from the paternal tradition in several obvious ways: First, Fritz deliberately sought proximity to political power; second, he consciously used the media spotlight and media strategies to position himself as a modern-day "chef" in direct opposition to his father. This was linked, third, to Fritz's political drift to the right. As a Catholic, August Thyssen had felt a natural affinity with the Center Party during the German Empire, even though he voiced far-reaching expansionist demands amid the nationalist exuberance of World War I. The Center's approval of the Treaty of Versailles in June 1919 was finally a good reason for both Thyssens to break with the party. Fritz henceforth found his political home in the DNVP, and later in the NSDAP.[5]

De Taillez points out that in the wake of the revolutionary postwar environment and the negotiation of the Treaty of Versailles, Fritz's relation to the media and his actions in the public started to change.[6] He gradually stepped out of his father's shadow, entered the glare of the inflamed national public sphere in a media-savvy manner, and adopted a right-wing conservative-patriotic political profile. The first instance of this was the spectacular arrest of father and son Thyssen by the Mülheim Workers' and Soldiers' Council on 7 December 1918—on charges of treason for years of collaboration with French big business. Not only did the arrest make waves in the media both nationally and worldwide, but the public now focused entirely on the person of Fritz Thyssen. August Sr.'s health was severely impaired. The hitherto all-dominant founder of the Thyssen Group fell virtually silent and retreated into the background. Fritz, on the other hand, took advantage of the unexpected public attention and now employed media strategies on his own behalf. Even the *New York Times* reported the incident on 10 December under the lurid headline "German 'Iron King' Seized by Socialists." By this, it meant Fritz, not August.

From then on, Fritz Thyssen distinguished between the confidential use of his social position and network, which required discretion and silence, and his public statements directed at the national and worldwide media. The American news agency Associated Press and international media such as the *New York Times* repeatedly mentioned him as one of the most prominent experts who rejected the Versailles terms for both national and economic reasons. Behind the scenes, however, Fritz behaved quite pragmatically. Even though he had personally tried to persuade individual members of the National Assembly to reject the Versailles Treaty at the last minute, he nevertheless actively participated in the confidential renegotiation of individual articles on behalf of the Foreign Office after it had been signed.

He also continued to work with Matthias Erzberger, who had been Reich minister of finance since June 1919, despite his father's public political break with the centrist. He did so in order to exert a pro-business influence internally on foreign exchange, credit, and raw materials issues. According to de Taillez, Fritz Thyssen was a "chief lobbyist for his own cause" who, whenever it seemed appropriate, specifically used the media to promote his interests.[7]

Figure 2.1. Trial before the French military court in the district court building in Mainz, 24 January 1923. Photo: Optische Anstalt G. A. Urmetzer Mainz. Fritz Thyssen standing in the dock, Franz Wüstenhöfer and Ernst Tengelmann seated next to him on the right. On the bench in the center, presiding judge Colonel Debeugny. At the round table r. defender Friedrich Grimm.

Fritz took his most decisive step into the political arena in 1923, after confidential negotiations between German mine owners and the French occupiers had broken down without any result. Through his protest stance in the "Ruhrkampf" (Ruhr struggle) which resonated widely in the media, he advanced to the status of national hero.[8] As spokesman for the Ruhr industrialists, he refused to obey the orders of the occupying forces to continue coal deliveries. Fritz Thyssen was arrested in dramatic fashion on 20 January along with five other mine directors[9] in the Bredeney town hall. The building was surrounded by armed French soldiers, a large crowd, and numerous domestic and foreign reporters. From then on, local publicity and the worldwide media were effectively in lockstep, until roughly seventeen thousand workers at the August Thyssen Hütte demonstrated the national solidarity of capital and labor in a twenty-four-hour strike. On 24 January, Fritz stood before a French military court in Mainz and was handed a fine,[10] while a nationally euphoric crowd of an estimated twenty thousand people sang

anti-France songs such as "Siegreich wollen wir Frankreich schlagen" (We will be victorious over France) and "Weh, o weh Franzosenblut" (Woe, oh, woe, French blood) in front of the courthouse.[11]

Before the flurry of flashbulbs from both domestic and foreign correspondents, the French occupying power likely regretted its decision to bring Fritz Thyssen before a tribunal, which now functioned as an international stage for his self-dramatization. He relished the media attention, for now he became a more visible and, what's more, a celebrated company leader. His father, on the other hand, resigned from the various mining boards of the Thyssen empire shortly after what transpired in Mainz—full of bitterness and with grave concern for his legacy.[12] The highly charged media coverage contrasted Fritz with his father, who was completely unmasked as a man all but incapable of acting.

Using sources, Felix de Taillez traced the path of Fritz Thyssen's media image from the Ruhr region to increasingly wider regional, then national and European, and finally international audiences. The media portrayed the entrepreneur as downright shy, modest, and awkward, yet firmly backed by the working class. The *Berliner Illustrirte Zeitung*, published by Ullstein, made him a national political star in its 4 February issue. The front page displayed his portrait in the manner of celebrity photography, with only his name underneath: Fritz Thyssen. The report framed him as a German Christ figure, the "new suffering hero of the people" who stood for the "immortality of a free Germanness (*Deutschtum*)" and who, along with many others, allowed himself to be "crucified for us and with us."[13] Other magazines followed suit, and the preferred medium increasingly became pictorial reportage.[14] The city of Hamborn declared Fritz an honorary citizen in January, and shortly thereafter a street was named after him for the first time in Aschaffenburg. On 19 February, he received an honorary doctorate from the Faculty of Law at the University of Freiburg; he continuously used the academic title thenceforth. He came to accept the fact that when his name and title were mentioned, the suffix "h. c." (honoris causa) was frequently omitted. Finally, a bronze medal was also minted with an inscription commemorating the "Räubergerichtshof" (robbers court) in Mainz.[15]

Simultaneously, there was a veritable international media frenzy surrounding the "national hero and martyr," while the Belgian-French counter-propaganda, which sought to expose him as an exploitative mining baron and a profiteering big capitalist, fizzled out altogether. On 21 January, Fritz made it to the front page of the *New York Times* for the first time; the next day it declared him Germany's most popular man and subsequently a political prisoner. *The Times* from London followed suit and reproduced this celebrity portrayal, this time with Amélie presented as the modest woman at his side. After the passive resistance came to an end, the Thyssen group began to attract notice in the United States. Deferential terms circulated, such as "the Rockefeller of the Ruhr."[16] Fritz Thyssen transformed himself into a media-savvy, visionary business leader and, according to Yves Cohen, struck a chord with the zeitgeist. From the turn of the century, "L'idéal du chef, l'obsession du chef" emerged as the byword of the times—in politics, military, business, and the humanities alike.[17] Fritz, skillfully using the media, rode this wave. As de Taillez shows, the climax of the Fritz Thyssen's self-depiction as the "German Carnegie" was an international conference at Columbia University in New York in 1931. He appeared there before the German and international public as one of Europe's most important "economic leaders."[18]

But he also emerged from his father's shadow in another respect after the Ruhr conflict, namely, as a major industrialist who now sought political influence himself. His choice of legal counsel in Mainz already indicates his shift to the extreme right: Friedrich Grimm. Grimm, who completed his habilitation in Münster in 1921 with a thesis on the Treaty of Versailles and was admitted to the bar in Essen, made a name for himself as a fierce opponent of the Parisian agreements. His clients included major industrialists such as Stinnes and Krupp, but he also defended the *Feme* murderers and other anti-republican criminals like, during the Ruhr occupation, the Freikorps member and dynamiter Albert Leo Schlageter. Officially a member of the DVP until 1933, Grimm nevertheless met leading National Socialists early on.[19] Already at the beginning of February 1923, in lightning speed, he published the documents of the so-called "Thyssen Trial" in two parts with the Hermann Sack Verlag Berlin, and shortly thereafter by the same publisher in English and French.[20] The unannotated source edition, which included the French files in German translation as well as the trial transcripts, including pleadings and the verdict, culminated in the defendant's declaration: "I will not be forced to commit an act against my fatherland or a dishonorable deed." It is hardly conceivable that such a publication could have been published by Thyssen's defense attorney, and in several translations at that, without his consent. Fritz must have seen in this a medial weapon for putting himself and "his" trial at the disposal of the extreme right.

Thyssen's progression to Hitler's side and his role in the rise of National Socialism[21] were already hotly debated at the time. As later contemporary historical research has pursued this discussion, it need not be repeated here. It is known that Fritz made sporadic financial donations to the NSDAP from the mid-1920s onward, presumably in previously exaggerated amounts. In 1930, he further made possible the purchase and conversion of the "Brown House" in Munich's Brienner Strasse with a favorable loan, in which Thyssen's own Dutch Bank voor Handel en Scheepvaart again acted as the financial clearinghouse. From then on, Fritz also socialized privately with Hermann Göring. This brought Göring into contact with elite society, while it in turn introduced Thyssen to the *Gauleiter* Josef Terboven in Essen. All this happened outside of the limelight behind closed doors. The political change of sides only became public in January 1932. As de Taillez meticulously reconstructs, Thyssen helped Hitler in a maximally inflamed political situation to give his two-and-a-half-hour speech at the Düsseldorf Industrie-Club, the casino of the company bosses on the Rhine and Ruhr. Hermann Göring was also on hand. Unlike the usual evening lectures, the event took place in the largest hall of the Parkhotel in front of 650 attendees; left-wing demonstrators protested outside. In his brief dinner speech, Fritz publicly sided with the National Socialists, having just left the DNVP.

The political significance of Hitler's speech for the Nazi takeover remains controversial, but Fritz's mass-media endorsement of Hitler had an impact in Germany and internationally, not least thanks to Heinrich Hoffmann's publicity photographs of him, Hitler, and Göring. He also became more involved, for example, by assuming the costs of printing and distributing Hitler's speech, which was available as a brochure. He moreover visited the homes of high-ranking Nazi functionaries and, conversely, invited them to visit him at Landsberg Castle. But it was not until January 1933 that these meetings were publicized in the mass media. Before that, they had mostly taken place in closed and exclusive face-to-face gatherings. According to the NSDAP central file, Fritz did not join the NSDAP until May 1933. By contrast, his wife Amélie already became a party member with one of the later coveted low numbers on 1 March 1931, the day of the official opening of the "Brown House" as party headquarters. First, she was an individual member of the Munich Reichsleitung, then she transferred to the Ortsgruppe "Brown House" on 3 October 1932. A little less than a year later she was finally referred to the responsible Ortsgruppe Mülheim of Gau Essen.[22]

The Exclusive Circles of Heinrich Thyssen-Bornemisza

In contrast to this brother Fritz, who sought publicity, mass-media visibility, and political influence at the national level, Heinrich took a different stance.[23] Along with repeatedly experiencing the destructive flipside of the coin when it came to mass media, he also refrained as a matter of principle from making any public political statements. Furthermore, he moved within distinctive social circles characterized by his individual approach to his familial fortune. We have already discussed Heinrich's integration into the Austro-Hungarian aristocracy and his weakness for the jet set that frequented grand hotels and seaside resorts.

Drawing on de Taillez's media-analytical perspective, the following discussion addresses two of Heinrich's further, predominantly elitist social circles, which featured very specific rules and mechanisms of operation. At their core, these were comparatively closed face-to-face encounters in which separate media were used to communicate about them to a wider audience and broadcast them to the mainstream. Specifically, we are talking about the art collector scene and the horse breeder/racing community.

In 1906, shortly after his wedding to the Hungarian baroness Margit Bornemisza, Heinrich stood before the highest English civil court in London in the glaring spotlight of a global public. The US-born actress Marion Draughn had filed a lawsuit for the violation of a marriage vow. The proceedings were reported by the serious international papers such as the *London Times* and the *New York Times* as well as the headline-grabbing tabloid press. Heinrich had met the young woman at the end of 1903 during a visit to Daly's Theatre, and they began an affair, traveling together to Paris, the south of France, and New York. Thinking of his planned wedding, Heinrich then broke off the relationship. The trial, as de Taillez demonstrates, quickly escalated into a genuine media scandal, with reverberations extending as far as New Zealand. The transnational fury of the mass media collided with the exclusive world of the Austro-Hungarian aristocracy, endangering Heinrich's fledgling marriage and his still unstable status within the aristocratic community. He responded by withdrawing from the general public: Heinrich became increasingly "invisible," which was even more possible when he withdrew from the operating business of the Thyssen-Bornemisza group at the end of the 1920s. No longer, it could be inferred, did he need to perpetuate his image as "chef." He had ample wealth at his disposal to now move his activities into the closed elite circles of art collectors and horse breeders and to invest there in other types of assets than before, namely in paintings and thoroughbred racehorses. Nonetheless, building up an image was also paramount here.

According to de Taillez's research, Heinrich's experience with mass media was always negative. This was true in the wake of the scandals surrounding his glamorous second wife Maud and during the first and only public exhibition of his foundation's collection of paintings, the "Rohoncz Castle Collection," at the Neue Pinakothek in Munich from July to November 1930.[24] Heinrich made a point of presenting his collection with great solemnity and a great deal of money. For help, he turned to the director of the Bavarian State Painting Collections Friedrich Dörnhöffer and the gallery owner Rudolf Heinemann. He covered the high costs of transport, insurance, the necessary new wall coverings, and the very elaborate catalog. A collection, after all, only gains in reputation and thus in value if it is displayed at a prestigious venue. After the exhibition opened, the press estimated the value of the collection at the impressive sum of 50 million Reichsmarks. Heinrich handled the printing of posters, gave interviews, and personally did the PR to get the word out about to the public. The opening turned into a media event; museum directors and art dealers from all over Europe showed up, as did the international, national, and local press and trade journals.

However, Heinrich was then reminded of how the mass media can unleash an uncontrollable and destructive dynamic. At the end of July 1930, the long-smoldering *Expertisenstreit* (as the contemporary quarrel over authentifications in art was called) unexpectedly erupted at his exhibition:

Out of the blue, it was suddenly stated publicly that about one hundred painting attributions were false. Once again, Heinrich had to bear the brunt of a media scandal that reached far beyond the expert public. The attacks were in fact part of a campaign targeted against the thriving expertise-and-attribution industry and largely engaged in anti-Semitic slander. Although the specific accusations against the Rohoncz Castle Collection soon proved mostly unwarranted, this correction no longer reached the wider public. Heinrich's attempts to use the media to manage the scandal, with the help of the press office of Düsseldorf's mayor Robert Lehr (DNVP) among others, also show that he had no qualms politically about the right, even if his contacts in this case were to no avail. Subsequently, Heinrich withdrew himself from Germany altogether, taking his collection of paintings with him. He took refuge in the seclusion of Villa Favorita on Lake Lugano, which he

Figure 2.2. Maud Feller, c. 1933. Photo: Moseseo, Nice.

had acquired in the meantime. He moreover sold the controversial paintings and restructured the collection, establishing the basis for its current global renown. It was not exhibited in public again during his lifetime. Unlike his brother Fritz, Heinrich also made himself completely invisible politically: while settling in Switzerland, he pledged in writing to the authorities that he would not engage in any political activity.

In Villa Favorita, on the other hand, Heinrich collected not only art but also the victory trophies of valuable racehorses. Under the incisive title "Passion, Prestige, and Politics," Felix de Taillez illuminates the initially exclusive milieu of horse breeding and gallop racing to which Heinrich retreated after the debacle surrounding his exhibition in Munich.[25] Although stables had already belonged to the estates of Rohoncz/Rechnitz Castle, befitting Heinrich's rank, he did not utilize them to pursue breeding or sporting ambitions. In 1926, after the death of his father, he chose racehorses as an investment for the first time. He launched this venture under the name "Stall Landswerth"—probably an allusion to Landsberg Castle. But Heinrich did not invest in horse breeding to any great extent until 1933. In the fall, he bought the Erlenhof stud farm near Bad Homburg with sixty thoroughbred horses and almost four hundred acres of land. In doing so, he acquired, beyond the immediate financial investment, social and symbolic capital in the contemporary yet still very elitist scene, which boasted its own publications, rules, and customs. Whereas Boris Gehlen's study analyzes the business model of the stud farm within the thematic scope of the research network,[26] de Taillez illuminates how in the peculiar subculture of horse breeding and equestrian sport the victorious thoroughbred horse not only achieved the highest level of media visibility but even mutated into a medium itself. In contrast, the owner customarily takes a back seat to the horse, the jockey, the trainer, and the stud and remains mostly out of the media eye. Just the same, every insider and aficionado knows his identity. Baron Heinrich Thyssen-Bornemisza was "one of them," and not infrequently seen in person on the turf in top hat and tailcoat.

It is known that Heinrich acquired Erlenhof through one of his Dutch asset transfer companies. He did so under extremely favorable conditions from the bankruptcy estate of the insolvent Jewish entrepreneur Consul James Moritz Oppenheimer from Frankfurt. He thereby came into possession of high-quality breeding horses whose offspring won prestigious trophies year after year. Erlenhof developed into the leading German racing stable in the 1930s. This highlights another dimension of horse breeding and horse racing, which is likewise part of Heinrich's wealth transfer. Admittedly, the acquisition of the stud was not a blatant act of Aryanization—Oppenheimer had fallen victim to the maelstrom of the world economic crisis. Nevertheless, under National Socialism, a new, powerful network of relationships developed between the Nazi rulers and equestrian sport so that the latter was "increasingly functionalized, but also ideologized."[27]

On the one hand, the connection to National Socialist racial thinking is evident in the breeding philosophy by which—as Simone Derix puts it—the horse's body becomes a treasured repository of desirable characteristics. It was not only for the SS that the horse bore a special significance in this regard.[28] On the other hand, horse breeding and equestrian sport adapted very quickly to the new political circumstances. The National Socialists, for their part, wanted to open elitist equestrian sport to the "Volksgenossen" (compatriots) and staged this new popular association with great publicity. For example, they sponsored the "Brown Ribbon of Germany," a new high-stakes horse race that was held every summer from 1934 to 1944 in Munich-Riem, near the main SS riding school. It was a flat race over twenty-four-hundred meters for three-year-old and older horses as part of the "International Riemer Rennwochen" with over twenty other flat and steeplechase races. The "Hauptstadt der Bewegung" (*Capital of the National Socialist Movement*)," which unlike Berlin and Hamburg lacked a top-class horse race, did not miss the opportunity to stage the event more lavishly with each passing year. The driving force was the former horse groom, horse dealer, and later cab and bus entrepreneur Christian Weber. An active and powerful early confidant of Hitler, he had been a member of the NSDAP city council in Munich since 1926 and floor leader since 1933. Weber took over as president of the local racing club in 1934 and successfully steered large municipal grants into its empty coffers every year. Equestrian sports became part of a deliberate image strategy in Munich. Integrated into a city festival week with races, parades, summer festivals, and all kinds of performances, the Nazi leadership gathered in Munich for all to see.[29] One such event was the nationally known "Night of the Amazons," which took place in Nymphenburg Palace Park from 1936 to 1939.

Thanks to his winning racehorses, Heinrich Thyssen-Bornemisza was integral to this Nazi network of relationships in horse racing. The same applies to Richard Kaselowsky from the Dr. Oetker entrepreneur family with his Ebbesloh stud farm.[30] Yet unlike the latter, Heinrich did not enter directly into the Nazi network of political and economic power; rather than being a politically active part of the propaganda machinery, he stayed passive. In the 1930s and 1940s, his horses won the prestigious Deutsches Derby at Hamburg-Horn four times, the Schwarzgold-Rennen four times, and the "Preis der Diana" at Berlin-Hoppegarten twice. In fact, through his "Wunderstute" (wonder mare) Nereide, who won one high-stakes prize after another in 1936, Heinrich was closely linked to the "Brown Ribbon" in Munich. In the extravagantly orchestrated Olympic year, the prize money had

Figure 2.3. The "Brown Ribbon of Germany" as a media event, Munich-Riem, 26 July 1936. Photo: "Tachyphot," Franz Hoffrecht u. Sohn, Berlin. In the middle after his victory, jockey Ernst Grabsch on Nereide. At the tail end, in top hat and tailcoat, probably Heinrich Thyssen-Bornemisza.

been specially increased to 100,000 Reichsmarks, making it Germany's most well-endowed race. The Deutsche Reichspost even issued its own commemorative souvenir sheet on 22 June with a 42+108 *pfennig* stamp, which many stamp collectors still consider the Reich's most beautiful souvenir sheet edition.[31] On 26 July 1936, Nereide won this trophy, too. The National Socialists promoted her victory as a national media event since the German mare had beaten her favored French rival. And its owner also emerged for the first time from his virtual invisibility, which is the norm in racing circles. While the horse's trainer, Adrian von Borcke, received the "Brown Ribbon" from Göring himself, Heinrich Thyssen-Bornemisza and his jockey, SS-Sturmführer Ernst Grabsch, whom photographers captured giving the Hitler salute after his victory,[32] received the Brown Ribbon gold medal. The baron allowed himself to be photographed with various important Nazi functionaries, and the photographs were distributed throughout Germany. He thus became a visible National Socialist figurehead based on the animal's almost mythical exaltation. Hermann Göring, who had assumed the politically authoritative functions for the relevant equestrian sport and breeding associations since the Nazi seizure of power, congratulated the owner of the legendary horse by telegram the day after the victory. The two had met at the track beforehand and were photographed together several times. They also had financial ties: Göring kept his bank account with August-Thyssen-Bank until his demise. This bank originated from von der Heydt's Bank AG in Berlin in 1930. Heinrich's Bank voor Handel en Scheepvaart had taken over its share capital in 1928 in order to completely reorganize it and use it for the financial transactions of his group of companies and the Thyssen family.[33] Although Heinrich, unlike his brother, did not get directly involved with the National Socialists politically, and although the relationships and contacts he cultivated in Villa Favorita suggest he was no Nazi ideologue,[34] he nevertheless showed no reservations about appearing in NS circles. Indeed, he played his part in the political-social transformation of the formerly insular and elitist world of horse breeding and racing. For the wartime period, Thomas Urban has elaborated in his study of forced labor in selected companies of the Thyssens of both lines that they were involved in the Nazi "labor deployment" system but did not differ fundamentally in this respect from other firms and corporations: "There is accordingly nothing unique to Thyssen."[35]

Figure 2.4. The baron as a poster child for the National Socialists. The "Brown Ribbon of Germany," Munich-Riem, 26 July 1936, photo: "Tachyphot," Franz Hoffrecht u. Sohn, Berlin. From left: Christian Weber, NSDAP floor leader in Munich city council; trainer Adrian von Borcke; owner Heinrich Thyssen-Bornemisza. Note also the wearers' distinctive hats.

Out in the Open: Fritz Thyssen, the Media, and National Socialism

De Taillez's study convincingly demonstrates Fritz Thyssen's media appropriation by Nazi propaganda after 1933,[36] in the course of which his likeness even found its way into a popular photo series of cigarette cards. His image oscillated between "friend of the working class" and "economic leader" and was closely linked to the political ambitions of Terboven, the *Gauleiter* of Essen in the Ruhr. Based on this web of relationships, which was also bolstered by the media, Fritz seems to have considered himself a kind of economic dictator of the west. In reality, the new rulers increasingly restricted his media options in the centralized press landscape until he was reduced politically to "a trophy hunter."[37] He accumulated titles and offices, which, however, were strictly ornamental (e.g. member of the General Council of the Economy, of the Prussian State Council, of the Academy for German Law). De Taillez describes how Fritz bought into a "media illusion," firmly believing for a remarkably long time in his rising influence in the Third Reich. Similarly, the international press was dazzled by the straw man and perceived Thyssen as a close friend of Hitler's and an economic dictator, if not as a strongman behind the Führer. The growing political distance between the two, however, is already manifest in the divergent media coverage of Thyssen's sixtieth and sixty-fifth birthdays in 1933 and 1938, which de Taillez construes as "propagandistic consolidation points."[38]

Fritz Thyssen stood in the spotlight of the media during his escape from Nazi Germany in 1939 until the definitive consolidation of his postwar image in 1959. With varying degrees of skill, he sought to use the media to influence the international public.[39] In this "battle over interpretive sovereignty," his hands in the Reich were tied. First, the uniform German press kept the subject of Thyssen under wraps; later, when information about the seizure and then confiscation of his assets leaked out, commentary only received the scantest of media attention. In the research network, Jan Schleusener has meticulously examined Fritz Thyssen's expropriation and the restitution of his assets after the end of the war.[40] In terms of the media-historical context of interest here, it is striking that the regime rarely went beyond using the *Deutscher Reichsanzeiger und preußischer Staatsanzeiger*, which published official personnel matters and administrative decrees. In February 1940, it also eventually reported on the revocation of the German citizenship of Fritz Thyssen and his wife. Prior to this, he had been stripped one by one of all the offices and titles he had held, albeit without this being brought to the attention of the German public and exploited for propaganda purposes. He forfeited his party membership, Reichstag mandate, state council title, honorary citizenship, and honorary doctorates. Thyssen's traces were silently erased wherever possible. Thus, in February 1941, the party-official examination commission for the protection of Nazi writing had his name removed from a conversation encyclopedia. Fritz Thyssen was thereby made "invisible."

The situation was quite different in the international public sphere. De Taillez reconstructs the "media itinerary" of the fleeing couple as the result of the mechanisms of an international, highly sensationalized news market whose logic determined the scope and rhythm of Thyssen's actions as much as the Nazi regime's. It becomes clear that the couple's flight across Europe took place on a worldwide media battlefield, where opposing parties keenly watched and reacted to each other very much according to strategic and tactical rules. Rumors, fabrications, and contradictory information played a key role. The Nazi rulers would not tolerate a steel magnate addressing the world public, even during the successful blitzkrieg phase. The Foreign Office and the Reich Ministry of Propaganda were thus quick to react: they corrected false reports and intervened diplomatically in Switzerland, which generally prohibited refugees and emigrants from engaging in political activities of any kind to avoid friction with the Reich.

Fritz Thyssen attempted in various ways to take control of his messaging and to redefine his international image. Not surprisingly, he was most concerned with setting the record straight on his motives for supporting National Socialist policies in the past and rejecting them now. Consequently, he personally contacted the press agencies, gave interviews, and arranged photo opportunities to effectively put a face on himself as a prominent refugee. In a major media offensive, he launched his letters of protest to the Nazi leadership in translation in the world's most widely read print media, including *Life*, *Sunday Express*, and *Paris-Soir*. In the end, he even wanted to become a book author (using a ghostwriter) and to explain his role in a global self-branding campaign (*I Paid Hitler*).

The international press and its extensive pictorial reports virtually created "a new type of emigrant" with the prominent refugee family. Narratives fluctuated between the early financier of the NSDAP, the "nationally minded business leader," ("nationaler Wirtschaftsführer") and Thomas Mann's Buddenbrooks' famous narrative of the rise and fall of a wealthy family.[41] Above all, it is apparent that Thyssen was now no longer able to win and maintain interpretive sovereignty. Much to the contrary: the more "authentic" the evidence was that he presented (documents, memoirs), the more the reins slipped. He eventually turned to a wayward professional ghostwriter in Emery Reves, who served both as press agent for Churchill and "editor" of Rauschning's (mostly fabricated) conversations with Hitler.

De Taillez pursues this interpretative thread in Fritz Thyssen's postwar life, demonstrating that it was also largely determined by his struggle to regain control over his public image—if under a different guise.[42] Much as he— and after his death his wife Amélie—fought to recover his fortune, there was also an effort to rid his name of the stench of fervent Nazism. This included attempts by some witnesses linked to the family to characterize him as an utterly apolitical, naïve person with good intentions.[43] The discussion about the authenticity of *I Paid Hitler* was only one of the media battlefields where now no longer Fritz Thyssen himself but his defenders around his widow and the Cologne lawyer Robert Ellscheid were busily engaged. The campaign continued beyond Fritz's passing: the positive staging of "Thyssen" in obituaries, in the burial in the family vault at Landsberg Castle in 1953, and in the deliberate, and highly successful, creation of a posthumous media image by the loyal Ellscheid resonated with the work of the Fritz Thyssen Foundation for the Promotion of Science and Humanities, founded in 1960. But as the reporting on the foundation's founding already shows, there were limits to Fritz Thyssen's public rehabilitation. While the German press tended to emphasize Thyssen's break with the regime, the foundation namesake's Nazi past cast a shadow over the international media landscape. Thus, the way in which Fritz Thyssen's contradictory life is remembered depends on the context.[44]

Notes

1. Gajek and Kurr, "Reichtum," 21–25; Derix, "Grenzenloses Vermögen," 169, 181.
2. De Taillez, *Bürgerleben*, 21, 30.
3. Review by Lesczenski, in H-Soz-Kult, 10 May 2018 (https://www.hsozkult.de/publicationreview/id/reb-24079).
4. Unless otherwise stated, the following is taken from de Taillez, *Bürgerleben*, 63–94.
5. See also Lesczenski, *August Thyssen*, 257–80; Eglau, *Fritz Thyssen*, 77–84.
6. De Taillez, *Bürgerleben*, 63.
7. Ibid., 70.
8. In detail, ibid., 71–94.
9. These were the general directors Wilhelm Kesten, Franz Wüstenhöfer, Ernst Tengelmann, Walter Spindler, and the mining assessor Hermann Olfe.
10. With one exception, the other defendants received higher fines than Thyssen (5,100 francs), e.g., Kesten 15,632 francs, Spindler 47,752 francs, Olfe even 224,066 francs; cf. Grimm, *Kriegsgerichtsprozess*, 95.
11. According to an observer from the Mainz city administration, quoted in Eglau, *Fritz Thyssen*, 17.
12. August Thyssen to Heinrich Thyssen-Bornemisza, 21 March 1923, in Rasch, *Briefe*, 180.

13. *Berliner Illustrirte Zeitung* no. 5, 4 February 1923, 83, quoted in de Taillez, *Bürgerleben*, 76.
14. Cf. ibid., 76f., with examples from the "Zeitbilder" supplement of the liberal *Vossische Zeitung* and the *Illustriertes Blatt* from Frankfurt.
15. Cf. ibid., 84f.
16. *New York Times*, 12 April 1923, 4, quoted in ibid., 86.
17. Cf. Cohen, "Chefs," 67f., 70f. (quotes); cf. in detail, idem, *Siècle*.
18. De Taillez, *Bürgerleben*, 225–41.
19. Grimm (1888–1959) continued his career in the "Third Reich" and in the Federal Republic. Cf. the excellent Wikipedia biography. He is one of the contemporary important jurists who are hardly known today.
20. Grimm, *Kriegsgerichtsprozess*, quote 21.
21. Unless otherwise stated, the following is taken from de Taillez, *Bürgerleben*, 299–376.
22. Hockerts, *Erbe*, 24f.
23. Unless otherwise stated, the following is taken from de Taillez, *Bürgerleben*, 51–61.
24. Cf. also Gramlich, *Kunstsammler*; unless otherwise stated, the following is taken from de Taillez, *Bürgerleben*, 119–58.
25. Unless otherwise stated, the following is taken from ibid., 158–88.
26. Gehlen, *Thyssen-Bornemisza-Gruppe*, 323–32.
27. De Taillez, *Bürgerleben*, 162.
28. Derix, "Rennpferd."
29. For more details, see also Rabe, "Hauptstadt."
30. Cf. Finger, Keller, and Wirsching, *Dr. Oetker*, 109–11; Finger, "Lebenswelten," 94f. Kaselowsky was also interested in purchasing the Erlenhof stud farm but then withdrew; see also Gehlen, *Thyssen-Bornemisza-Gruppe*, 325.
31. https://www.briefmarken-sieger.de/braunes-band-1936-briefmarken-block-gestempelt-katalog-nr-621-bl-4-deutsches-reich/ (retrieved 26 March 2021).
32. Cf. photograph in Rabe, "Hauptstadt," 171.
33. See also Wixforth, *Stahlkonzern*, 200–202.
34. Gramlich, *Kunstsammler*, 276f.
35. Urban, *Zwangsarbeit*, 163.
36. Unless otherwise stated, the following is taken from de Taillez, *Bürgerleben*, 334–76.
37. Ibid., 353.
38. Ibid., 365–68 (quote 365).
39. Unless otherwise stated, the following is taken from ibid., 377–476.
40. Schleusener, *Enteignung*, here esp. 51–134.
41. De Taillez, *Bürgerleben*, 390, 409 (quotes).
42. Cf. ibid., 463–75.
43. Cf. ibid., 456.
44. Cf. in this regard Hockerts, *Erbe*, 146f.

CHAPTER 3

THE THYSSENS AS ART COLLECTORS
Investment and Symbolic Capital (1900–1970)

(Johannes Gramlich, 2015, 2nd ed. 2021)

Why would members of a family of entrepreneurs acquire art collections, some having international renown, over three generations? Do they not just collect different things, but collect differently? Are there distinguishable "types" of collectors? What connects family, art, and commerce? Johannes Gramlich's investigation[1] stands at the intersection of a transnational history of art, business, family, and contemporary events, drawing on sources from more than thirty German and international archives. He demonstrates how the peculiar link between aesthetics and economy opens fascinating insights from the analytical perspective of family and fortune. For although the art market functions according to the logic of capitalism, the price of a work of art is not entirely independent of its artistic value. Moreover, the acquired object is not merely art or a commodity; it's a form of investment and thus also an object of speculation. During the times of unstable currencies and uncertain investment opportunities caused by the deep political and economic crises of the first half of the twentieth century (the Russian Revolution, two world wars, inflation, world economic crisis), art ownership was considered an appropriate means to secure mobile capital.

Following French sociologist Pierre Bourdieu, Gramlich defines the artistic field as a "market of symbolic goods," in which an art collection represents an objectified form of cultural capital. Acquiring and building an art collection always opens opportunities for prestigious image cultivation and self-presentation. In his brief philosophy of collecting, Manfred Sommer formulates it this way: "By not only observing, but at the same time displaying, [the art collector] exposes himself. . . . In showing the object, he also always presents himself; and he makes himself vulnerable . . . by vouching for the visual import of his object of interest (*verbürgt sich für die Sehenswürdigkeit seiner Sehenswürdigkeit*)."[2]

Therefore, Gramlich's initial thesis is that it was precisely the diversity of art's uses that made it a much sought-after collection item for the Thyssens:

Figure 3.1. Amélie Thyssen in front of the painting of her late husband Fritz in the Dreischeibenhaus ("Thyssen-Hochhaus") in Düsseldorf, 1965. Photo: Bernd König. To commemorate her husband, Amélie Thyssen wears a diamond-studded heart pendant around her neck, something she was often depicted with.

collecting art was a means of self-representation and social distinction; it served to enhance their image among the economic elite as well as among broader segments of the population; it was an investment and a lucrative asset; it was a tool of value creation and appreciation; it was a means of saving taxes or circumventing foreign exchange restrictions. Additionally, it was well suited to preserving a lasting public memory of its collector beyond death. The interplay of these potential uses and profit opportunities that art offers the collector is (also) what made it so fascinating for the Thyssens. Gramlich succeeds in elaborating different "collecting logics" and different weightings of motifs for the individual family members to reveal the Thyssens' collection strategies and to distill different "collector types."

Gramlich's investigation, praised by experts as an "excellent case study,"[3] therefore focuses less on the art-historical significance of the collections than on the Thyssens' actions on the art market and their self-staging as collectors. By buying and selling art, they entered as financially powerful actors the arena of collectors, gallery owners, auction houses, dealers, and agents. This included their unscrupulous representatives, to some of whom the Thyssens fell prey. In terms of time and content, the emergence of a global art market and its cross-border cash flows coincided with the creation and expansion of the Thyssen-Bornemisza collection and other art collections belonging to the family, some resulting from divisions following death or divorce (e.g., Fritz Thyssen collection, Bentinck-Thyssen collection, Carmen Thyssen-Bornemisza collection). The expertise that developed in the family was also closely linked to the emergence of a differentiated international system of art experts, who, for instance, appraised and authenticated works by unknown artists, determined the value of art, or established the principles for restoring damaged artworks. This includes, not least, media involvement, if not the principal constitution of the art market by a large number of art magazines.

The fault line, which separated August Sr. from his children because of notable differences in their approach to wealth, also ran through the field of art collecting. All the Thyssens, after all, owned or collected art. The furnishing alone of one's own residence with artistic objects makes significant contrasts clear, and even more so the creation of an art collection.

The "Bourgeois Standard Case": August Thyssen Sr. and Fritz Thyssen

August Thyssen Sr., whose art holdings are documented only in fragments, was hardly active on the art market, for as a company founder, he simply lacked the time.[4] He certainly did not seek better access to the world of artists and did not join any art associations.[5] Nevertheless, he adorned his residence with works of art, very much in keeping with the "bourgeois standard case."[6] Accordingly, the private home was to be furnished in a manner befitting the status of its owner, i.e., also artistically. At August's death, the inventory after all listed sixty paintings. Following convention, portraits played a major role. They decorated the staircase and the study, signifying identity, tradition, and power. Two groups of images are striking here: portraits of rulers and statesmen as well as family members or oneself.

It befits the mindset and lifestyle of the company founder that he deeply revered Otto von Bismarck, the founder of the German Reich. At Landsberg Castle, he displayed no less than two portraits of Bismarck: an original Lenbach, acquired in 1911 and positioned prominently in the entrance hall, and an anonymous copy modeled after Lenbach, acquired as early as 1900, located in his study. When he gradually had to relinquish control of the company, August started to compare himself with the "great Reichskanzler." Indeed, as he wrote to Fritz, "the founder of the great German Empire . . . had also been treated in an equally ruthless and unworthy manner by the young emperor." Here one might quietly add: just as he felt treated by his sons. Consequently, he did not acquire a portrait of Kaiser Wilhelm II for his private rooms, whereas a portrait of Wilhelm I hung in his study.[7]

The study and salon were embellished with many portraits of individual family members, paintings, and photographs, but above all several high-quality artistic depictions of himself. From paintings to busts, no expense was spared.[8] For his eightieth birthday, August Sr. had six hundred postcards made with a portrait photograph.[9] He also pursued his own commemoration policy as founder not only of the Thyssen enterprises but also of a family dynasty. Art was utilized in family circles as a "tradition- and identity-building element." Accordingly, in his will he established Landsberg Castle, including its works of art as a foundation, as a place of family identification that was not to be divided up, not to be sold, and, quite to the contrary, to be occupied and used as often as possible by the family.[10]

In one respect, however, August Thyssen broke with the bourgeois norm in his dealings with art, and that was in his relationship with Auguste Rodin. Since the late 1880s, Rodin had been regarded as the most renowned sculptor in the international art world.[11] August Sr. presumably approached the sculptor in Paris through his friend, the Berlin banker and art collector Karl von der Heydt, and Rainer Maria Rilke, Rodin's secretary in 1905/6. Gramlich manages to show that the Thyssen companies chief executive used his purchases, initially three sculptures in 1905 and four more in 1908, specifically as part of an image campaign to expand his ventures in France. There, German investment was perceived as a continued annexation by economic means. In the spring of 1906, the otherwise so publicity shy company head specially invited the French journalist Jules Huret from Le Figaro to Landsberg Castle. On this occasion, the publicist discovered, as if by chance, the first two newly arrived Rodin sculptures in the conservatory. The aim of the initiated profile story turned out to be successful: Huret spoke positively about the owner's artistic acumen in his article, which was published a short time later in book form in both French and German. Afterward, August never made his Rodin sculptures public again. He did, however, display the thoroughly erotic sculptures in plain view in the conservatory, where his business partners and occasional guests could also admire them.

Gramlich shows that Fritz Thyssen's attitude toward the purpose of art was initially not very different from his father's.[12] He was only interested in the socially appropriate decoration of the interior of his home, which, according to convention, served as a private retreat for the family and the center of bourgeois socializing and representation.

It was not until the 1920s, in the wake of inflation and currency reform, that he also discovered the function of art as a capital investment with stable value. However, he deviated from his father in five crucial ways.

Unlike the unsociable founder of the company, Fritz was, first, very disposed to social gatherings. In his home, eminent figures of the art world and the leading representatives of business and politics, including Hitler and Göring during the Nazi era, came and went, contemplating the works of art on display. In Fritz Thyssen's case, the connection between art and representation is especially clear. As Gramlich emphasizes, works of art continued to be important symbols of status and power in the twentieth century.

Figure 3.2. Landsberg Castle conservatory with marble sculptures by Auguste Rodin, around 1910. Photographer unknown.

Second, Fritz followed the unwritten rules governing wealthy lifestyles: it was now "proper" to collect art systematically, and Fritz, in contrast to his father, also explicitly cultivated his self-image as an art collector. He compiled an exquisite collection together with his wife Amélie, refraining, however, from scholarly completeness. Collecting, however, remained "an important peripheral activity on the fringes of his entrepreneurial and political commitments."[13] Therefore, although he was well aware of the profit opportunities on the art market, he did not adopt any strategies to increase the value of his own art objects, unlike his brother Heinrich during the same period. For this reason, he had a catalog of his art holdings printed in 1926 with the help of the renowned Finnish art historian Tancred Borenius, but in an edition of only five copies for purely private use.[14] Fritz Thyssen moreover consistently rejected the idea of making his collecting activities known beyond a limited circle.

Third, Fritz was himself active in the art market, where he operated quite independently. By 1939, he had acquired sixty-six paintings and numerous valuable porcelains and sculptures. While he maintained close contacts with renowned art and antique dealers at home and abroad, his visits coincided with business or private trips. For him, the notion of traveling just for the sake of art was remote. However, Fritz Thyssen was involved in art politics in a narrower sense, albeit within a limited sphere. For example, he was a patron of the Landesmuseum in Bonn and joined the board of the "Haus der Deutschen Kunst" in Munich, thus making a politico-cultural statement on the side of the National Socialists.

Fourth, in contrast to his father, who always openly confessed that he knew nothing about art, Fritz acquired a solid knowledge of art history through self-study, which by now was considered good form. When his assets were confiscated by the National Socialists in 1939, the library of "Haus Thyssen" comprised over eleven hundred art history monographs, catalogs, and periodical volumes, which were divided among several academic libraries in the Rhineland. Fritz approached art dealers and museums knowledgeably and exercised his own judgment, while Amélie also read specialized literature. As is typical of the descendants of a successful business founder, Gramlich explains, they transformed "economic capital into cultural capital"—for the "expansion of their own horizons" and cultivating their self-image.[15]

Fifth, Fritz and Amélie followed the bourgeois conventions of their time, meaning they collected "typical" things like old porcelains and tapestries. But they also acquired paintings, goldwork, and furniture. Another area of collecting, rather unusual today, also fits into the art trends of the day: distributed throughout the rooms were sixteen late Gothic wooden sculptures, some up to 190 centimeters high, with religious subjects (Madonna and Child, figures of saints, praying people). As art historian Matthias Weniger points out, art collectors would never again have such an interest in late Gothic sculptures as in the decade between 1900 and 1910, and prices skyrocketed.[16] Fritz Thyssen actively participated in this artistic trend through his buying and collecting behavior. Yet, amid the predominantly Protestant Ruhr industrialists, the Thyssens' Catholic faith came to the fore.[17] Christian themes from the fifteenth century also stood out among the paintings in "Haus Thyssen," including a Botticelli, a Ghirlandaio, and a Perugino. As a result, the entrance hall and—in keeping with the gender stereotypes—the boudoir had a certain "sacred flair." Overall, then, the furnishing of the country estate with art objects combined "Christian, feudal, and bourgeois elements." It did not feature any modern or contemporary art and was thus strongly influenced by conservatism—it was much more conservative, at any rate, than Landsberg Castle with its erotic Rodin sculptures. Gramlich used photographs, letters, and other sources to reconstruct the furnishings of the Thyssen couple's living quarters. In this way, he provides a revealing glimpse into the conservative bourgeois domestic culture of the German business elite in the German Empire, the Weimar Republic, and National Socialism.

Collecting as Vocation:
Heinrich and Hans Heinrich Thyssen-Bornemisza

The most extensive art collection of international renown from the Thyssen family, the Thyssen-Bornemisza Collection, has been on display in its own museum in Madrid since 1992; the largest part was acquired by the Spanish state. Its genesis shows the strategic and professional approach of its originators. Heinrich, who had been investing heavily in the art market since the 1920s—and in this he differed from his brother and even more so from his father—regarded himself as a professional art collector. Until World War I, he too still viewed the primary purpose of art as lying in the adornment of the social and living rooms of Rohoncz Castle in a manner befitting their status, just as they already were. Louise Price, the couple's mother-in-law, who lived in the same household, later explained that Heinrich's renovations were aimed at technical modernization, while preserving the old representative interior with stucco ceilings and ceiling frescoes.[18] A surviving photograph shows a wood-paneled suite of rooms, the floors carpeted with sumptuous armchairs, an expansive fireplace with sundry art objects on the mantel (an antique clock, two candelabras, a vase), numerous large paintings on the walls, and hunting trophies in an adjacent room.[19]

After moving to the Netherlands, however, Heinrich began to invest in art with a different self-image starting in the second half of the 1920s.[20] He continued to furnish his residences with art objects as a matter of course, including his more-or-less permanently occupied suites in the grand hotels. This was also quite common among other high-net-worth individuals. At the Esplanade in Bellevuestraße, for example, which was located on the mile of the Berlin art trade, Heinrich's neighbor in the next room was the banker Eduard von der Heydt, who had already acquired a valuable collection of paintings. Art dealers rented space to hold art auctions at the hotel. Hotel life essentially revolved around art. The 1920s and early 1930s were generally a good time to invest in art. In the aftermath of the Russian Revolution, the market was virtually flooded with art from the estates of the Russian nobles who had fled. A similar effect was triggered a little later by the Great Depression, when ruined collectors threw their collections on the market at knockdown prices in order to remain solvent or become solvent again.

It was during this time that Heinrich took the decisive step toward professionalization. By 1930, he had purchased a verified 261 paintings from 27 art and antique dealers, including two he particularly trusted: Goudstikker in Amsterdam and Fleischmann in Munich, one of the oldest art houses in the Bavarian capital. He set about this boldly and confidently, without any permanent advisors or agents. Much more so than his brother Fritz, he amassed an astonishing amount of expertise. The library in the Villa Favorita comprised fifteen hundred volumes, some of them very old and precious. When it came to the attribution of a painting, he also attached great importance to written authentications from respected experts and often had up to four expert opinions prepared.

Heinrich also benefited from his intensive networking with respected art dealers and scholars. He called on the best experts, who were always very influential (among others, Rudolf Heinemann, Max Friedländer, Friedrich Dörnhöffer). At the same time, he remained active in the background and thus nurtured the image of the quiet art lover and passionate collector for whom the acquisition of works of art was deeply personal. Gramlich devotes special attention to these networks, which Heinrich as well as the other Thyssens built up around their collecting activities. In doing so, he can reconstruct an important part of the contemporary art market. Heinrich entered this milieu as a demanding, idiosyncratic customer who preferred to travel across Europe in person rather than making purchases from his office. The art dealers were kept in line by his financial clout as Thyssen-Bornemisza. In short, no one could afford to lose him. Gramlich analyzes the many intertwined reasons that motivated Heinrich to invest his fortune in art. The canonization of the Old Masters through the subject of art history at the universities stabilized the market value of old art, which made it a safe investment from an economic perspective. On the other hand, contemporary art took on (and still takes on) the characteristics of a speculative asset. Heinrich invested exclusively in Old Masters and, although to a much lesser extent, in nineteenth-century art. He rejected modern art. Personal taste and the pursuit of a stable investment coincided here, notwithstanding the fact that even then Heinrich's collection was tinged with an air of the old-fashioned and conservative.

Heinrich also went about professionally increasing the value of his collection. Until 1930, he was hardly visible on the art scene and effectively known only to insiders. Still, the art magazines whispered of a "big buyer" on the European art market. At auctions, he was represented by art dealers, and only occasionally did he make one or two paintings available on loan for special exhibitions. When he did, however, it was at exquisite venues such as London's Royal Academy, the Royal Museums in Brussels, the Düsseldorf Kunstverein, or The Hague Kunstverein. Just as was the case later in the equestrian scene, Heinrich, abiding by the codes of the art collectors' community, discreetly faded into the background as an individual. As lender, the catalogs listed the "Rohoncz Castle Collection." With the first (and during his lifetime last) large special exhibition in the Munich Pinakothek in the summer of 1930, which then unexpectedly culminated in the media scandal surrounding expert opinions,[21] Heinrich embarked on a strategy to increase the value of his collection. From the catalog, its scope and artistic focus and thus Heinrich's profile as an art collector are obvious. He presented 428 paintings, including 361 Old Masters and sixty-seven nineteenth-century masters, as well as eighty-eight objects from the areas of sculpture, furniture, arts and crafts, and book miniatures. Heinrich's preferences were likewise made clear: Dutch and Flemish masters predominated, followed by Italian, German, and French painters.

Heinrich added other specific motifs that remarkably adhered to educated middle-class principles. From the beginning, he intended to build up his collection according to art historical criteria and to compile a museum collection oriented toward the major international art museums. It was almost as if he had the pedagogical aim of fulfilling a civic educational mission. He was committed to documenting the course of European art history and to providing a representative overview of the entire European art scene from the Middle Ages to the nineteenth century. To guide a broad public through art history, he firmly rejected a request to present only a selection of his collection in the Munich Pinakothek. He even insisted on determining the hanging of the pictures himself according to scholarly criteria. People came in droves: sixty thousand art lovers visited the special exhibition and bought almost five thousand catalogs at three Reichsmarks—no small feat in times of global economic crisis. Heinrich consistently presented himself in the catalog as a proselytizing art connoisseur, national benefactor, and patron of the arts. His calculation worked: after the opening of the exhibition, the respected art historian Max J. Friedländer wrote in the widely read journal *Kunst und Künstler* that the "stunningly universal" show was the fulfillment of the "dream of a German museum director" who "lacked the resources to realize his ideal." Tancred Borenius, who had cataloged Fritz Thyssen's collection only four years earlier, simultaneously announced in the *London Times*, i.e., in front of an international audience, that it was "an encyclopaedic illustration of European painting" to which "nothing comparable" currently existed.[22]

Such a great number of paintings, which Heinrich named the "Rohoncz Castle Collection" with aristocratic aplomb, could of course no longer simply be hung up privately, even for a Thyssen-Bornemisza. From the start of his collecting activities, therefore, the question of the collection's location always came up. Until the exhibition, Heinrich had stored most of his paintings in the warehouses of various art dealers, meaning that no one, not even their owner, could view them. The exhibition at the Pinakothek was therefore also the first opportunity for Heinrich to personally see his extensive collection in one place. Despite all the interest in increasing its value, this again puts the motivations of a collector in a different light. Previously, all efforts to assemble the collection in the forthcoming prestigious "August-Thyssen-Haus" in Düsseldorf, which was to house the administrative headquarters of the Thyssen-Bornemisza group, had failed. The plan had partly encountered great resistance with the urban elite of the Rhine metropolis.

Heinrich's decision to build a new, ultramodern corporate headquarters in the middle of Düsseldorf and to house his art collection on the second floor reveals another rationale for investing in art. Indeed, August Sr. had already recognized that it was one of many elements of a family identity formation that sought to establish a tradition based on a dynastic narrative. A much-hated father during his time and cause of endless conflict, he thus mutated into the founding figure of an entrepreneurial family dynasty.

The plans for the new building, however, were not realized due to Heinrich's withdrawal from the operational business at the head of his group of companies. Art collecting itself now became an intergenerational tradition that bound the whole family together.

The acquisition of Favorita on Lake Lugano was therefore, as Gramlich shows, the solution to a whole series of problems. At long last, the painting collection could now be housed in a unified setting and, after the Munich scandal, assembled in a new and highly professional way. Heinrich also had a well-known architect build a gallery adjacent to the villa, which provided space for a large part of the collection on three floors in what were probably twenty-six rooms.[23] The move to Switzerland also brought him considerable tax savings. In October 1932, he negotiated a remarkable deal with the cantonal authorities of Ticino, according to which he set the value of all his capital in Switzerland and abroad at only 1 million francs. In addition, the

Figure 3.3. Heinrich Thyssen-Bornemisza (third from right) in the Villa Favorita gallery, 1947. Photo: Christian Schiefer, Lugano-Paradiso.

property on the lake was 1.75 million francs, at an annual taxable income of 50,000 francs! At the time, the tax policy in Switzerland, according to which the taxes to be paid were based on wealth and income, was extremely lucrative for the very wealthy.

The question of whether there was Nazi-looted art in Heinrich's collection is easier asked than conclusively answered. It would require thorough research on each individual object and the meticulous reconstruction of its provenance, which was beyond the scope of the project. In principle, the acquisitions made after 1945 by Heinrich's son Hans Heinrich, who transformed and supplemented the collection to the quality that the Museo Thyssen-Bornemisza in Madrid displays today, could also be tainted. Based on the following observations, Gramlich arrives at the tentative conclusion that Heinrich Thyssen-Bornemisza at least did not deliberately or systematically seek to profit from the Nazi persecution policy or the Nazi art looting. Three reasons support this finding: First, Heinrich acquired a considerable part of his collection already before 1933, between 1928 and 1930. Second, he was living in Switzerland from 1932 and, unlike before, was subsequently active primarily in the Swiss and US art markets. Unquestionably, Nazi-looted art circulated there as well, but not to the same extent as in the German Reich. Third, with the intensification and systematization of Nazi persecution and confiscation policies from 1938 onward, as well as with World War II, the circulation of Nazi-looted art on the European art markets in fact increased dramatically. But by that time, Heinrich had already largely ceased his collecting activities. His 1937 catalog can be considered a kind of terminus of his collecting efforts, for after that Gramlich could only prove very sporadic acquisitions. Indeed, during the particularly critical period from 1938 to 1945, Heinrich Thyssen-Bornemisza was scarcely involved in the art market.

After Heinrich's death in 1947, the collection fell to his children. His son Hans Heinrich was appointed sole heir, and compulsory shares fell to Gaby Bentinck, Margit Batthyány, and Stephan Thyssen-Bornemisza.[24] The distribution of the inheritance reveals two things: Unlike in and between the generation of the father and grandfather, it was free of conflict. Borne by the will for peaceful sibling relations, there was not sibling rivalry but brotherly and sisterly comity.[25] Second, the generational change in the Thyssen-Bornemisza family once again revealed a significantly different way of dealing with assets or art. Hans Heinrich followed different principles than his father in multiple respects.[26] He actively entered the public sphere with the Villa Favorita picture gallery as early as 1948 and, from then on, made it permanently accessible to the public. Once again, it is possible to observe the powerful effect of tax motives. With the pending new tax agreement, the canton of Ticino pursued a different policy than it did formerly with Heinrich. The authorities were no longer willing to downgrade the value of the unique collection if it were not open to the public. Hans Heinrich undertook this step and at the same time obtained his sought-after Swiss citizenship in 1950—until then he had held Hungarian citizenship, which no longer offered any advantages in times of the escalating East-West conflict. Nevertheless, the Swiss treasury was satisfied with another low valuation of the collection. The negotiated amount was 1.2 million francs. Ultimately, the authorities were concerned that the collection might be withdrawn from Switzerland.

It was only after this deal, during the 1950s, that Hans Heinrich became active as a collector on the art market. Now, he was even more energetic, independent, and in the public spotlight. He strove to make up for the losses of paintings resulting from his siblings' inheritances.[27] After a faltering start, he grew perfectly into his new role as an increasingly glamorous art collector and was a constant presence in the international media. On balance, Hans Heinrich ended up investing even more in art than his father did. Between 1970 and 1978 alone, he spent a total of more than 170 million francs, and by the end of the 1980s, he had expanded the collection to more than 1,500 paintings.[28]

The criteria he used to develop the art collection are important, as they provide insight into Hans Heinrich's strategies for setting and increasing the value of his fortune invested in art. To start with, they stand in contrast to the image that prevails today. Extant inventory lists show that by the end of

1960, in addition to inheritance losses, Hans Heinrich had parted with a further 60 paintings that did not meet more demanding quality criteria. Indeed, the critical voices surrounding the exhibition at the Neue Pinakothek in 1930 had not been entirely unfounded. Around 80 works were added during the same period. In 1960, the collection comprised only 369 paintings, 150 fewer than when his father died. However, the collection was now considered to be of superior quality. All the new acquisitions were Old Masters, mainly from the Netherlands of the seventeenth century. According to Johannes Gramlich, "in 1960 [the collection] can be described as even more conservative than it had been before," since the works that were disposed of were mostly from the nineteenth century and hardly replaced. By the mid-1970s, Hans Heinrich sold another 65 paintings, which were also not considered to be of great value. Now, only 225 of the original 520 paintings in his father's collection were still in his possession. Along with other new acquisitions, the Old Masters now formed a stable core of 370 paintings.[29]

Johannes Gramlich establishes that the triad of family, art, and business is especially apparent in Hans Heinrich and his conspicuous lifestyle. In the same way that Hockerts observed how Amélie Thyssen virtually acted as "trustee of her late husband's wishes" to rehabilitate his name and that of the Thyssen enterprises,[30] Heinrich's son was also unmistakably concerned with keeping the name of the Thyssen-Bornemiszas free of any association with National Socialism. With his inherited art collection, Hans Heinrich vigorously pursued an image policy that benefitted the family and the company. It was thus no coincidence that he significantly increased his financial investments in art from 1955, when the Allies decided to unfreeze the German companies from the Thyssen-Bornemisza group after the Dutch ones. The collection now appeared under the name "Thyssen-Bornemisza." Unlike his father, Hans Heinrich was very present in the management of his group of companies, and he used his art collection for an internal image campaign. For instance, from the late 1950s onward, he had magnificent illustrated books with high-quality color plates of his collection produced and gave them as gifts to important business partners and customers. The first such volume, published in 1958, had a print run of 7,000 copies and cost him the then enormous sum of 146,000 German marks. In 1964, 7,500 copies of a second illustrated book with works from the Italian Renaissance were printed; this cost the owner around 128,000 francs. A third extravagant volume from 1969 was also used as an advertising vehicle. Hans Heinrich further organized exhibitions of the collection, bearing his family name, within the company. The first such exhibitions were held in Rotterdam and Essen in 1959/60; he also lent individual paintings to his companies to decorate their premises. In addition, he arranged for loans to leading museums worldwide, which were instrumental to increasing the value of his collection.

Finally, he used the special exhibition of his collection at the National Gallery in London in 1961, which had global appeal, as a promotional tool to finally break free of the narrower regional context. It was a unique opportunity, because until then the National Gallery had never showcased a private collection. Hans Heinrich selected 118 paintings with an estimated value of 18 million US dollars, including mainly Old German masters, which were underrepresented in London. The primary goal of the exhibition is reflected in the list of catalog recipients: leading international figures from the worlds of politics, business, and art, including President Lübke, Chancellor Adenauer, Princess Margaret of York, and the kings of Greece and Sweden. Likewise, the guests invited to the exhibition opening were of the highest international standing. The public-relations aim of the exhibit was underlined by the preface of the catalog. Referring to the tradition of Thyssen-Bornemisza as art patrons, it further stated that father Heinrich had recognized early on the fateful disaster caused by Adolf Hitler and the National Socialists and distanced himself accordingly.

Yet the exhibition in the National Gallery is also interesting in another respect. Immediately afterward, Hans Heinrich began to invest specifically in classic modern art such as expressionism and surrealism, which his father had firmly refused to do. After World War II, the appreciation of modernism in the West became a social, almost political, necessity around the world. A collector thereby demonstrated his unequivocal rejection of National Socialism and its destructive art policy, but also of Soviet artistic dogma. In the Federal Republic too, modern art, and here above all abstract art, was regarded almost doctrinally as transparent, democratic, and anti-totalitarian. This is evidenced by the exhibition history of the Kassel documenta, which took place around the same time.[31] In this context, Gramlich observes, collecting modern art was simultaneously "a political statement for freedom, individualism, and democracy." Whereas companies had previously decorated their representative rooms with the Old Masters, this yielded to an almost ostentatious preference for modern and contemporary art. Beyond its political symbolism, it was associated with "creativity, a sense of innovation, and dynamism."[32]

Accordingly, Hans Heinrich's collecting behavior not only had to do with his own artistic preferences but was also part of his strategic effort to increase the value of the collection and to keep up with the—increasingly glamorous—spirit of the times. Unlike his father, who preferred seclusion and remaining invisible to the media, Hans Heinrich sought the limelight. He often liked to show up at auctions, which became veritable media events, and had himself profiled in international art magazines. By August 1981, he owned well over seven hundred modernist works; he was frequently at Sotheby's and Christie's, as well as at international art dealers specializing in modernism. Even though he had never lived in Germany or been a German citizen, he acquired a prominent, international reputation as an "anti-Nazi." That said, the name Thyssen and its enterprises were still too closely associated with a now incriminating past from which he, like other members of the Thyssen family, sought to disentangle himself with a certain zeal. Collecting art thus constituted a way of dealing with wealth that was as characteristic as it was skillful and could be used in a variety of ways. As Gramlich concludes, art held "immense potential for the Thyssens across the generations, which could be harnessed for diverse purposes."[33]

Notes

1. Unless otherwise stated, the following is taken from Gramlich, *Kunstsammler*, 11–55.
2. Sommer, *Sammeln*, 64.
3. Review by A. Schulz, *Vierteljahrschrift für Sozial- und Wirtschaftsgeschichte* 103 (2013): 380f.
4. Gramlich, *Kunstsammler*, 57.
5. Unless otherwise stated, the following is taken from ibid., 57–113, 365f.
6 Ibid., 57.
7. August Thyssen to Fritz Thyssen, 15 January 1924, in Rasch, *Briefe*, 271.
8. Cf. Gramlich, *Kunstsammler*, 75, ill. 2.
9. Cf. Rasch, "Bau," 289.
10. Gramlich, *Kunstsammler*, 368f.
11. For more details, see ibid., 85–105, 365f.
12. Cf. on the following, unless otherwise stated, ibid., 113–95.
13. Ibid., 366.
14. Borenius, *Haus Thyssen*. A copy of the catalog, long thought lost by the family, was discovered during the project's research in the library of the Art History Institute of the University of Bonn, cf. Gramlich, *Kunstsammler*, 114. In 1986, the Bavarian National Museum in Munich was to exhibit the Fritz Thyssen Collection in public for the first time; cf. Württemberg, *Sammlung*.
15. Gramlich, *Kunstsammler*, 129.
16. Weniger, *Oppenheim*, 1f.
17. On the following, Gramlich, *Kunstsammler*, 122–26 (quotes 123, 126).
18. Derix, *Die Thyssens*, 149; Gramlich, *Kunstsammler*, 197f.
19. Cf. photograph in Rasch, *August Thyssen*, 70.
20. Unless otherwise stated, the following is taken from Gramlich, *Kunstsammler*, 195–279.
21. Cf. also de Taillez, *Bürgerleben*.
22. Gramlich, *Kunstsammler*, 214, also 243f.
23. On the opening of the private gallery in 1936, which was postponed several times, see ibid., 273–76.
24. On the back and forth about the Rohoncz Castle Collection foundation and Heinrich's will, see in detail ibid., 291–303.

25. Ibid, 298.
26. Unless otherwise stated, the following is taken from ibid., 303–47; summarized, see also 370, 375.
27. After the siblings' settlement, Hans Heinrich inherited more than three hundred paintings from old masters and about thirty from artists of the nineteenth century; cf. ibid., 301.
28. Ibid., 311, 370f.
29. Ibid., 311f., 317f.
30. Hockerts, *Erbe*, 33, also 53, 67, 124–28.
31. Cf. Warnke, "Gegenständlichkeit"; Guilbaut, *New York*.
32. Gramlich, *Kunstsammler*, 336f.
33. Ibid., 375.

PART II

CORPORATE HISTORY PROJECTS
Selected Findings

Why Thyssen? On the State of Research and the Research Problem

The Thyssen group was one of the most important industrial conglomerates in Germany in the late nineteenth and twentieth centuries, and the Thyssen family was one of the most prominent industrial dynasties. While the Thyssens are an important part of economic history—especially in heavy industry—they were also involved in many other areas.

Nevertheless, when the research project was launched, little was known about them and their companies. This was probably because the Thyssen enterprises were so heterogeneous and underwent so many changes. The records, moreover, were scattered among many domestic and foreign archives of companies, state, and business institutions and Thyssen family members.

True, there are several studies on the origins and early history of the group up to around the death of its founder August Thyssen, including the work by Jörg Lesczenski on the *Wirtschaftsbürger*.[1] But less was known about the development of the companies after his death in 1926. At that time, the inheritance was divided: The largest heavy industrial share was passed on to the eldest son, Fritz Thyssen. A heterogeneous mix of other companies went to the third eldest son, Heinrich Thyssen-Bornemisza.[2]

For a long time, the steel sector outshone the other Thyssen businesses. Then came the decline of heavy industry in the Ruhr region from around the 1970s onward. Little was known about the businesses of the Thyssen-Bornemisza branch. More recently, a series of accounts and editions was published by long-time group archivist Manfred Rasch. Occasionally, attention has also been paid to individual business units and separate, often particularly spectacular topics such as the colorful and contradictory life of Fritz Thyssen.[3] On the whole, however, previous research on Thyssen's corporate history was meager. Above all, there was usually a lack of reliable studies based on archival sources that meet the standards of modern business history and entrepreneurial research. For instance, the history of Vereinigte Stahlwerke AG (Vestag) under National Socialism was only known heretofore in rudimentary detail. It was however the largest German steel group, and the most important heavy industrial piece of August Thyssen's legacy was incorporated in it. Alexander Donges thus made this the subject of his study on "corporate policy between market economy and state economy" in our research network. Critics hailed it as a "bonanza" (*Glücksfall*).[4]

Donges here examines the company's ownership structure, corporate governance, business development, and investment policy.

Regarding our knowledge of forced labor at Thyssen, there were similar deficits. In a study conducted by our network and supplementing the work of Donges, Thomas Urban therefore investigated forced labor at Thyssen in World War II. He focused on the steelworks and rolling mills in the Duisburg area, which were part of Fritz Thyssen's Vestag, along with companies owned by Heinrich Thyssen-Bornemisza: two shipyards in Bremen and Flensburg and the coal mine *Gewerkschaft Walsum* near Dinslaken.

As already mentioned, the Thyssen-Bornemisza corporate structure was also the least researched and largely unknown. In their studies on the "Baron-Konzern" and the Thyssen-Bornemisza Group (TBG),[5] Harald Wixforth and Boris Gehlen thus broke new ground. Their primary point of departure was corporate governance. They inquire into the shaping of corporate policy, in particular regarding the management style, leadership, and control structures against the backdrop of the political, legal, and economic-social conditions.

In the media, politics, and journalism, "Thyssen" was not infrequently a foil for people's hopes, desires, criticism, and hostilities. It was often pressed into service—or allowed itself to be taken into service—by a variety of vested interests. Appropriations were evident in the arrest of August and Fritz Thyssen by armed members of the Mülheim Workers' and Soldiers' Council on 7 December 1918; in the public adulation of Fritz Thyssen for his resistance to the French in the Ruhr occupation; in the resonance to his support for National Socialism; in the impact of his radical public break with National Socialist leaders in 1939; in the representation of Thyssen's Ruhr enterprises after 1945 as icons of reconstruction, economic recovery, and reconciliation with France; and, finally, in the success of the European Economic Community. Also not conducive to an impartial understanding and discussion of all things "Thyssen" was the fact that the family repeatedly assumed an extravagant role before the public and was frequently at the center of scandals—from the divorce of August and Hedwig Thyssen in 1885 to the glamorous public lives of family members to the numerous divorces.

Figure P2.1. Fritz Thyssen. Painting unsigned and undated, before 1926. Collotype, in: Tancred Borenius (ed.), *Haus Thyssen: Die Sammlung* (Berlin, 1926, private print), vi.

Bearing all this in mind, our research network set itself the goal of carrying out historiographical investigations. We intended to explore unknown terrain based on archival material that had not yet been assessed. Evaluating new sources from Germany, Europe, the United States, and Argentina is an enormous undertaking. The ten studies in the publication series, with the thematic title "Family—Company—Public Sphere: Thyssen in the 20th Century," attest to this.

Of course, there is also a methodological claim here, namely, to integrate the connection between company and family history over the long term. Each volume is prefaced by an editorial that sets out the aim of the project as a whole: to bring together a family history inspired by cultural studies with a corporate history perspective, focusing on the maxims, strategies, and practices of corporate management. Furthermore, the approach applies to Thyssen's network of foundations, holdings, and individual companies, etc., for the purpose of corporate development, asset preservation and increase, and, finally, the use of available political, legal, social, and other options. It was decided that special attention should be paid to the period of National Socialism. What's more, in terms of corporate history, we must of course consider the context of economic history, specifically, the question of typology and specificity. As a heavy industrial conglomerate, the company was closely involved in general economic policy and development (demilitarization, rearmament, dismantling, regulation, liberalization, Europeanization, and incipient globalization, etc.). It both benefited and suffered from these trends. Regarding the formulated research problem, what do the sources reveal? What reliable findings can be identified?

In company or entrepreneurial history, the most important questions are: What was the orientation and nature of entrepreneurial performance? What factors determined behavior? Was it possible to respond to challenges, to be resilient, to ensure, to be successful? If so, how? And if not, what was the reason for failure? It is well-known that there are very different types of entrepreneurs: the technician, the businessman, the communicator, the managing heir. What characterized the Thyssens? What motives and maxims guided their actions? What structures and processes did they test out or establish? What caused success and failure? These questions, first of all, relate to the operational side of the business: the organization of procurement and production, sales and administration, dealings with employees, etc. They also concern the "external realm": relations with competitors, trade unions, and, above all, the state.

In the research network as well as within the corporate history focus of the research project, we had exhaustive discussions about which theoretical approaches or explanatory models would be fruitful for the respective studies. The network analysis that proved so productive in the family history portion of the project was also closely examined in the corporate history work. Among other things, a special workshop was held with experts in network analysis in the social sciences to explore whether and, if so, how we could make this approach useful for studies with a focus on corporate history. It became apparent that a network analysis in the narrower sense of the social sciences, which could quantitatively determine and graphically depict exchange relationships, would generally not be possible due to the peculiar logic of the entrepreneurial topics and the respective source situation. This applies to any number of business considerations and decisions, such as questions of profitability and risk diversification. The situation is different regarding family and entrepreneurial, operational, and political and other activities. Here, the inclusion of theoretical, conceptual, as well as practical network considerations is naturally required and was done wherever feasible.

Theoretical approaches of the new institutional economics proved to be particularly helpful for the analysis and explanation of the decisions, rooms for maneuver, path dependencies, etc. For instance, the transaction cost theory explains the existence and the success of enterprises by the fact that they can produce transactions more economically than these could be acquired on the market. Moreover, the principal-agent approach analyzes the dilemma of the unequal interests and access to information between principal and agent and possibilities for overcoming it.[6] Admittedly, our studies were not conducted to test the usefulness of an economic explanatory model. The latter rather serves in the background to organize the material and to understand the constellations and developments—to make them plausible and, if possible, to explain them. In this regard, theoretical approaches such as the network and the principal-agent approaches, the question of transaction costs and path dependency, etc., are helpful.[7] They cut a swath through the heterogeneous, contradictory, and often chaotic reality. On the other hand, they are often unable to adequately capture the specifics of the respective individual cases. Therefore, in each of the six subprojects on corporate history, the methodological approach is selected that is most appropriate to the topic and promises the greatest analytical gains. If necessary, it is combined with others.

On the Company's Development

Before delving into the topic further, a concise outline of the company's development is necessary. August Thyssen had established the conglomerate in the nineteenth century, and during the period of high industrialization had turned it into a diversified company and one of the most important and largest on the Rhine and Ruhr. The company focused on the extraction of pig iron and steel and the manufacture of intermediate products for further processing, as well as the mining of coal and the production of coke for energy supply. This was supplemented by related production areas, logistics, and capital supply. Thyssen had built up an empire that included coal mines, metallurgical plants, foundries, rolling mills, machine factories, transport companies, shipyards, gas and water supply, and the energy industry, as well as—with a particular focus on the Netherlands—trade, logistics, and financial services.

After the death of the founder in 1926, the inheritance was effectively split into two areas. Over time, each took on a life of its own, even if they were initially interwoven in many ways. Most of August Thyssen's iron and steel companies were absorbed into Vereinigte Stahlwerke AG, the previously mentioned new giant conglomerate of German heavy industry, which only few major companies in the sector did not join. Thyssen had been preparing this before his death because he did not trust his children to successfully continue his work. His eldest son Fritz was supportive of the plan, but his third eldest son Heinrich was skeptical. The heavy industrial legacy was under the aegis of Fritz Thyssen, who assumed a leading role in Vestag. After his break with the National Socialists in 1939, they confiscated his property. During the world war, the armaments business was especially profitable. After 1945, Vestag was demerged by the Allies. Following difficult, protracted disputes, the German steel industry was relaunched with the support of the German government and federal states, with Thyssen playing a major role. As the postwar period progressed, however, the companies' capital requirements increased to such an extent that Amélie, the wife of owner Fritz Thyssen, who died in 1951, and his daughter Anita were unable to meet them. Consequently, the family lost more and more of its significance in and for the company, which became a publicly owned corporation in the late 1960s. In the context of our research network, the development of "Thyssen" in the Adenauer era with the resurgence of the corporation and the fading importance of the entrepreneurial family is the subject of Johannes Bähr's study *Thyssen in der Adenauerzeit*.

To a certain extent, a "spin-off" of the demerger was one development that led to the establishment of the Fritz Thyssen Stiftung. In the wake of the restitution and the fresh start of Thyssen's steel activities—and not least in memory of Fritz Thyssen—his wife and daughter set up a foundation. Soon, it would become one of the most important institutions in the Federal Republic for the promotion of science. Hans Günter Hockerts tackles this subject in his study (*Ein Erbe für die Wissenschaft*) as part of our research network.

Figure P2.2. General view of August Thyssen-Hütte, 1924. Photographer: unknown.

Returning to the dismantling of August Thyssen's empire: most of the companies in his estate that were not transferred to Vestag fell under the aegis of Heinrich Thyssen-Bornemisza. August's third son had married a Hungarian aristocrat in 1906. He subsequently let himself be adopted by his father-in-law, acquired Hungarian citizenship, and, in 1907, received the hereditary title of "Baron Thyssen-Bornemisza von Kászon" from Emperor Franz Joseph I. This change of citizenship proved time and again to be important—and mostly advantageous—for Thyssen-Bornemisza's inter- or transnational entrepreneurial activities as well as for securing his assets amid the political turmoil of the twentieth century.

He now tried to efficiently combine the heterogeneous parts of his inheritance while centrally managing them as a group—mostly from the Netherlands since 1919 and from Switzerland since 1932. His companies were based in numerous countries. When he died in 1947, he was succeeded by his son Hans Heinrich Thyssen-Bornemisza (1921–2001), then the latter's son Georg Heinrich Thyssen-Bornemisza (b. 1950). After a series of turbulent times, the Thyssen-Bornemisza Group (TBG) today remains a successful internationally active business group.[8] In our research network, this history was investigated by Harald Wixforth for the period from the death of August Thyssen to 1932 (*Vom Stahlkonzern zum Firmenverbund*) and by Boris Gehlen for the subsequent period up to the mid-1950s (*Die Thyssen-Bornemisza Gruppe: Eine transnationale business group in Zeiten des Wirtschaftsnationalismus*).

Company and Family

The company's success gave and continues to give the family relevance and prominence. By the same token, the family helps provide the company success and stability, especially by contributing assets in their various forms, not only monetary ones, and trust. In the case of Hedwig Pelzer, the wife of August Thyssen, her fortune was critical to the early economic success of Thyssen's ventures. Family and company are thus interdependent and intertwined. The same could be said even more pointedly for the Thyssens' money and power: the family used the fortune, but the fortune also "used" the family. It created not only opportunities for taking action but also dependencies, expectations, and powerful constraints. This began at the latest with the usufructuary shackles that August and Hedwig Thyssen put on their children when they divorced—an elementary, disastrous containment of the children in a gilded cage that limited their options for decades. Such dependencies continued after the death of August Thyssen in the difficulties of dividing up the parts of the company, variously interwoven in terms of ownership, operation, and function, in a meaningful and practicable way among the heirs. Heinrich and Fritz constantly depended on each other and their mutual good will for subdivisions and sales as well as for votes in joint enterprises until the end of the inheritance settlement, a period of around ten years. This was further expressed in the interconnectedness of the (family) foundations, which forced the Thyssens to resolve or overcome their respective attachments and conflicting interests in a cooperative manner. The inheritance not only brought the descendants into conflict but also forced them together; it required them to reconcile tensions and negotiate disagreements.

Family businesses are the oldest and still the most widespread type of business. They are particularly adaptable (among other things, by adopting niche strategies) and oriented not to quick profit but long-term success, sustainability, and dynastic continuity. In this respect, they strongly resemble the aristocracy. Through the socialization within the family, the family-run business effectively passes on its entrepreneurial deliberation and decision-making culture, which it has learned over generations, to the children "at the kitchen table." Family businesses are, of course, also especially vulnerable, such as when heirs are absent or unfit, when there is family strife, or when capital resources fall short.

With the creation of large markets through the industrial revolutionization of transport and thus sales opportunities and goods production, and with the triumph of capitalist methods based on the division of labor, the family business was often supplanted in the industrialized countries by anonymous, manager-controlled, market-based corporations. By no means, however, did it disappear or become obsolete—neither in the industrialized countries nor in the developing and emerging countries.[9] In Germany, the rest of Europe, and the United States, around 70 to 90 percent of all companies are currently family businesses. On average, they generate more than half of the respective national gross domestic product and are also increasingly international in their orientation.[10]

To be sure, the idea of a family enterprise primarily calls to mind rural, mechanical, hotel, and hospitality businesses, those small and middle enterprises (SME) that are the veritable "backbone of the German company landscape."[11] Family-owned companies can also be found among large companies and multinationals, even though their overall share is lower due to their higher capital requirements. In the case of large companies, especially if they are joint-stock companies, it is usually difficult to determine whether they are family businesses, because capital and management as a rule have been separated.

Roughly speaking, it was owner-managed family businesses starting in the nineteenth century that formed the prototype of the medium-sized company. As already mentioned, they were jeopardized by the age and death of the owner, by succession problems and family quarrels. On the other hand, they generally benefitted from the absence of the principal-agent problem and thus by lower transaction costs. Furthermore, they profited from a perspective of sustainability, continuity, adaptability, and flexibility, as well as (mostly patriarchal) employee loyalty and an intensive basis of communication and trust within the company.[12] Family businesses usually reacted to challenges arising from the increasing complexity of procurement and production, sales and administration, or from their own expansion with family or bureaucratic solutions—or a combination of both.

As a result of market growth, increasing capital requirements and ever higher demands on entrepreneurial knowledge and performance, the owners—to put it again in simple, illustrative terms—were initially supplemented and later replaced by managers. In his impressive studies,[13] Alfred D. Chandler has elaborated the transformation of the owner-run enterprise (entrepreneurial enterprise) into the manager-run enterprise (managerial enterprise) and the reasons for it. But he did so mainly with a view to large companies and thus in a one-sided manner.

Recent research, in contrast, uses multiple criteria and their combination in order to define whether it is the family, the banks, other actors (e.g., private equity, hedge funds), or "the market" that controls the company. The decision-making power in corporations can vary greatly, for example according to absolute majority, blocking minority, nested shareholdings, etc. It is moreover not uncommon for informal, personal constellations to have an impact on who holds or occupies a management position. It may suffice here to mention the distinction made by Mark Casson[14] between the family-owned firm and the family-controlled firm. In the former, the family owns enough shares to block competitors, while in the latter, it determines the chairman of the board. In the disputes over the restitution of Heinrich Thyssen-Bornemisza's assets, which had been confiscated in Great Britain and the United States during the world war, Anglo-American lawyers also drew on the concept of the beneficial owner. This was the person who owned the property and was able to benefit from it, even if he was not listed as the owner, e.g., in the commercial register.[15]

Trust—Capital—Assets

Regarding family businesses, emphasis must be placed on the great importance of the factors trust, capital, and wealth. Thus, the Rothschild banking house largely owed its rise and sustained success to the fact that the management of the businesses in Frankfurt, London, Vienna, Paris, and Naples was in each case in the hands of one of the five sons of founder Mayer Amschel Rothschild (1744–1812). The latter had stipulated in his will that all key positions in the company were to be filled by family members. Rothschild thereby laid the foundation for trusting and enduring cooperation between the various stakeholders and reduced the risk of the company being damaged by fraud, excess, and the like. In this way, he solved a principal-agent problem.[16] At Siemens, the situation was similar: company founder Werner von Siemens (1816–92) was based in Berlin, his brother Wilhelm headed the London branch, and his brother Carl the foreign operations in St. Petersburg.[17] Such examples are easily multiplied. It goes without saying that those who rely on their family do not always and unconditionally do so on secure ground. Nevertheless, with the support of family members, there is a better chance of getting a grip on the principal-agent problem. The same applies mutatis mutandis to consultants, operations directors, etc. Incentives typically played a role here, but trust remained indispensable.

A similar observation can be made in the procurement of monetary capital. Whoever receives capital from a bank loses autonomy. The bank is necessarily given the opportunity to control and co-decide—and credit institutions usually exercise this function professionally, rigorously, and unsentimentally. But for those who receive capital—in whatever form—from family members, the situation is different. Here, too, the recipient is not (or is no longer) entirely free in his entrepreneurial activities, but the influence has another form. Anyone who, like August Thyssen, can bring assets from his wife into the company does not—at least in this case—impair his ability to expand the company. Yet during the divorce, the problem of joint property arose—with far-reaching consequences. August Thyssen avoided the influence of banks in financing his entrepreneurial activities. Instead, he founded or bought his own bank. In their studies, Wixforth and Gehlen describe in more detail the problems that this created for Heinrich Thyssen-Bornemisza's group of companies.[18] On the one hand, there was the commercially defined and justified self-interest of the credit institution; on the other, there were the expectations of the companies in the group seeking credit.

"Wealth" is among the integral elements of family and corporate history. It is not limited to monetary capital but also includes cultural and other kinds of capital and the associated opportunities and authority to act. The perspective thus expands from the specifically economic to the broader cultural view. Like trust, any kind of fortune is also an economic factor. From the point of view of corporate history, the factor of economic capital is the main "asset." But there are also factors such as reputation, mystique, influence, etc., which are important for entrepreneurial action and the exercise of power. They (can) also contribute to success. Derix has unraveled the dimensions of "wealth" (Vermögen) and pointed out that, among the generations of heirs, the preservation of accumulated wealth became more important than an original (new) acquisition.[19]

Advisors and Consultants

Advisors and Consultants have always wielded great influence among the Thyssens. In the days of August Thyssen, it was lawyers and financial experts who gave advice on family disputes, divorce, inheritance contracts, property issues, etc. After World War II, this only intensified and took on a specific character. In connection with Fritz Thyssen's imprisonment and denazification proceedings, legal advice was now especially important. This was also true for the problems brought by dismantling, demerging, and remerging. In this context, and in view of public subsidies, antitrust issues, and other regulations in both the German and European contexts, political support also took on greater significance. This was all the truer since there was no longer a family member who had a guiding and supervisory role in the family business itself.[20]

The Thyssen circle of advisors was substantial. To begin with, it included the formally appointed consultants both inside and outside the company. Derix estimates at more than one hundred the number of those who advised on wealth-related problems due to family conflicts, relocation, and fortune protection between about 1910 and 1945.[21] The circle moreover included informal advisors, such as fellow entrepreneurs, association representatives, etc. The most important advisory group in Thyssen's history was doubtless the committee of four people who advised Fritz's wife Amélie and daughter Anita after his death. It included Robert Pferdmenges, multisupervisory board member, banker, and longtime friend of the Thyssen family; lawyers Robert Ellscheid and Kurt Birrenbach, asset managers for the two women; and Hans-Günther Sohl, head of August Thyssen-Hütte. They enjoyed the confidence of Amélie Thyssen, who kept a low profile in entrepreneurial matters she was not very familiar with. The possibility thus opened for the committee to make fundamental entrepreneurial decisions—albeit always with the consent and on behalf of the female owners. It was the latter who laid the foundation for the establishment of the Fritz Thyssen Foundation.[22] Trust played a critical role here. In recent years, behavioral economics has highlighted the importance of trust for decision-making.[23] Trust underpins communication and protects against

HERR SOHL:
 " UND ERST MAL DIE GANZEN KONZERNE ZUSAMMEN:
   NICHT ZU SCHLAGEN!"

Figure P2.3. Amélie Thyssen and Hans-Günther Sohl around 1960. Photographer unknown (photo portfolio in the possession of the Fritz Thyssen Foundation, Cologne).

uncertainty. In the relationship between Amélie Thyssen and the Thyssen committee, the hierarchy appears to have flattened, especially regarding Pferdmenges. A personal, emotionally anchored trust, which is occasionally attributed to premodernity, took hold that proved no less effective than institutionally supported rules-based trust.[24] Admittedly, such intimacy was not always in force. Moreover, no matter how important, familiar, or experienced the experts may have been, one fact loomed between them and the Thyssen family like an insurmountable glass wall. The advisors, namely, were not tied to the Thyssens either by marriage or kinship, nor by any resulting (and possibly intertwined) property claims. Advisors were to be sought, selected, consulted, and, in the event of conflict, removed. Everyone has family. You can even part ways with certain family members. Indeed, the history of the Thyssen family is full of such dissociations and distancing—but also of rapprochements. Usually, however, family members remain family members, even after a separation. This linkage fosters a sense of obligation. If the connection of wealth (see above) is added to the awareness of a common origin, a family bond, the distinction to the advisor is even more obvious.

To be sure, every specialist or advisor is superior to the advice seeker in the individual case. Thyssens' advisors likewise had power over them. Still, no matter what any advisor, expert, or confidant could bring to the table in terms of knowledge, qualifications, or symbolic wealth, it typically paled in comparison to the towering influence of the Thyssens' colossal fortune. Whether expert, external consultant, acclaimed specialist, or confidant, anyone could be shown the exit in the event of a conflict. This was true even for those in the highest positions and with the loftiest standing. Kouwenhoven, the longtime, experienced, successful director of Bank voor Handel en Scheepvaart, is a case in point: when he was suspected to be disloyal, Heinrich Thyssen-Bornemisza gave him a princely severance and sent him packing. Kouwenhoven, of course, never got over his dismissal.[25] Fritz-Aurel Goergen, head of the Thyssen company Phoenix-Rheinrohr, also had to leave in 1957, even though he was successful in his company. He was not as well connected as his adversary Hans-Günther Sohl, the chairman of August Thyssen-Hütte, and interfered with his plans.[26] Robert Ellscheid, the loyal, highly professional law professor, advisor, and representative of Fritz Thyssen in the denazification proceedings, suffered a similar fate. In 1949, he experienced "a positively hateful rejection" from his employer, the bitter, moody, erratic Fritz Thyssen, which forced him to resign his position. It was thanks to the efforts of Thyssen's wife Amélie and Ellscheid's noble posture that he returned and was willing to continue working for Thyssen. He proceeded to do so with great zeal and success.[27]

Thyssen and Thyssen-Bornemisza – Outlines of Success and Failure

The history of Thyssen's companies also reflects overarching developments in German as well as general economic history. In this sense, it concretizes, illustrates, and offers diverse examples of various trends. This is clearly shown in the studies themselves and cannot be adequately addressed here. However, it is worth highlighting some conclusions *pars pro toto*.

To what extent "Thyssen" was a "family business"—in the sense described above, it would be the key decision-maker, whether as owner, as a significant shareholder in the capitalization, or as the person providing or deciding on the chairman of the board—seems easy to determine at first. While this was the case with August Thyssen, it was no longer so for Thyssen's heavy industrial ventures when August Thyssen-Hütte became a publicly owned corporation in the late 1960s. This shift, however, did not occur in a straight line. The heavy industrial legacy lost its character as a family business when it was incorporated into Vereinigte Stahlwerke AG in 1926, even though Fritz Thyssen had significant influence there with his share of around a quarter of Vestag's capital stock and as chairman of the supervisory board. The influence came to an end in 1939 when he fled and his assets were confiscated.

After the world war, the situation was complicated. Fritz Thyssen received a 20.74 percent share in the Vestag successor companies in the demerger, but it was subject to sales requirements. As a result of the reorganization that followed, his two heirs together held between 43.4 and 53.9 percent of the capital stock in four successor companies in 1954. This meant that Hüttenwerke Phoenix, Rheinische Röhrenwerke, Niederrheinische Hütte, and Deutsche Edelstahlwerke were Thyssen family businesses. August Thyssen-Hütte can also be regarded as such. The joint capital share of Amélie Thyssen and her daughter was only 26 percent, but the management positions were closely linked to her family. These included supervisory board chairman Pferdmenges and executive board chairman Sohl. In addition, the share of ATH was increased to 52 percent by 1956. In 1955, the first two companies merged to form Phoenix-Rheinrohr; this company then merged with ATH in 1965. All the companies were Thyssen family businesses in the sense mentioned above. But since then, the capital share fell dramatically. In 1968, it was only around 25 percent (blocking minority); the family influence declined accordingly.[28] August Thyssen-Hütte was now a publicly owned corporation, not long after the death of Amélie Thyssen. The latter had seen "the reconstruction of a family-owned industrial group on the Rhine and Ruhr as an almost sacred commandment of the 'Thyssen tradition,'" whereas "her daughter showed no interest whatsoever in corporate policy matters."[29] The connection with the family finally ended completely when the Fritz Thyssen grandsons Federico and Claudio Zichy-Thyssen, Anita Zichy-Thyssen's sons, left the supervisory board of the group. They sold their stake in 1997—worth an estimated DM 1.2 billion—to Commerzbank. In the same year Thyssen Stahl AG merged with Krupp Stahl AG to form ThyssenKrupp Stahl AG.[30]

The Thyssen-Bornemisza conglomerate, on the other hand, appears to have remained owned and managed by the family to this day. Thus, although this initial "general store" was something of a historical accident "left over" after the separation of the heavy industrial sector (which was more compatible systematically and in terms of production technology), it proved to be the more durable of the two. The most important reasons seem to be the strategies that remained in place despite all the extravagance and idiosyncrasies of August Thyssen's son Heinrich and grandson Hans Heinrich Thyssen-Bornemisza: diversification, internationalization, and corporate governance geared to long-term and sustainable profit. A further factor was the proximity to political power. Fritz Thyssen supported Hitler for many years but then made a radical break. The situation was different with Heinrich Thyssen-Bornemisza: he, as well as his brother's heirs, benefited from political support after the war and the end of National Socialism. He ultimately won the support of the Dutch government in his post–World War II restitution claims. Fritz Thyssen took an entirely different course. His heirs, in contrast, had great success after World War II when they won the support of the German government for the restitution and further development of their heavy industrial activities. In both instances, network relationships were important, if not decisive—in the Dutch case, relationships based on kinship and friendship; in the German case, relationships based on trust and friendship. In each case, of course, the interests of entrepreneurs and politicians were also fully aligned.

Within the companies, there was a transition from owner-entrepreneur to manager-entrepreneur. This was part of an extraordinary trend caused by growing company size, complexity, and opacity, increasing demands on know-how and capital, etc., progressive internal division of labor and professionalization, and occasionally the disinterest and inability of owner-heirs. August Thyssen had largely relied on managers who had been brought up through the company and on whose loyalty he could count. He gave them plenty of latitude to act independently, rewarded them generously, and demanded results in return. His sons had continued in this vein both conceptually and in terms of personnel. With the transition to Vereinigte Stahlwerke, there were breaks in continuity regarding workforce and organization. After 1945, the situation was utterly new and different. Many older staff were now no longer active. Moreover, the industrialist's position was bleak: Fritz Thyssen was in the position of an expecting client, isolated from his workers, and ill. He died in 1951. His heirs, his wife Amélie and daughter Anita, had no experience running a company. With the new start after the end of the war, influence was gained by people who did not come from the former business environment but who were introduced to Fritz Thyssen by family members and through personal contacts.

The heavy industrial part (Fritz Thyssen's inheritance) was shaped by a series of special developments: the merger with Vestag meant that Fritz Thyssen was able to benefit from the new size, but he also suffered in terms of his own freedom to act. The expropriation of Fritz Thyssen that occurred in 1939 also necessarily strengthened the management layer. Following World War II, there was demerging and restitution. August Thyssen-Hütte was booming, and the consultants Pferdmenges, Ellscheid, Birrenbach, and Sohl gained exceptionally great influence. Fritz Thyssen's wife and daughter were unable to meet the growing need for capital, and the company eventually became a publicly owned corporation.

As for the Thyssen-Bornemisza part, Heinrich Thyssen-Bornemisza experimented for some time with the management instrument of a board of directors, but soon abandoned it. He then controlled the company from Switzerland insofar as he "governed from the cabinet," holding regular audiences. At first glance, this would seem like a retreat into private existence. But a closer look reveals that the business-minded and banking-savvy Thyssen-Bornemisza effectively and sustainably steered the winding paths of his ventures based on key figures provided by his accounting firm, Rotterdamsch Trustee's Kantoor (RTK).

After World War I, inflation, the stabilization of the German mark, and progressive internationalization in the 1920s, many business owners saw corporate mergers, the formation of trusts, and conglomerates as the ideal way to achieve synergy effects and regain, maintain, and improve the competitive position of their industry on international markets. This applies, for example, to heavy industry (e.g., the Stumm corporation in addition to Vestag) as well as to the chemical industry (e.g., IG Farben). However, the cost advantages from growth were not sustainable. The downside—including inflexibility and high costs due to repeated reorganization, etc.[31]—became apparent during the global economic crisis.

In keeping with the editorial maxim, particular attention was paid to the Nazi era. This is the focus of four of the six publications in the corporate history part.[32] Under National Socialism, companies went through a series of extraordinary developments as a result of the autarky policy, armaments economy, and considerably intensified regulation, as well as the expropriation—or "Aryanization"—of Jewish property. According to "our present knowledge, the Thyssen companies neither appropriated 'Aryanized' companies nor took over foreign plants in the occupied territories during the Nazi era."[33] However, the joint project's research revealed that Stephan Thyssen-Bornemisza, the eldest son of Heinrich (and brother of Hans Heinrich) Thyssen-Bornemisza, participated as a private individual in "Aryanizations" in Austria to invest his own fortune. Nevertheless, he was at the same time managing director of Seismos GmbH, which belonged to his father, and in this respect the Thyssen-Bornemisza group was marginally involved.[34] After 1945, the demergers, restitutions and the division of Germany established new conditions. As Donges has elaborated, the trend toward further processing was path dependent and part of the extraordinary trends in heavy industry. Thyssen, like many other heavy industry companies, expanded into downstream production stages, included semi-finished and finished products and incorporated companies for the supply of capital and transportation services/logistics.

After an initial industrial internationalization in the late German Empire, internationalization took place in four phases in the twentieth century. It began with the opening of national economies after World War I—which, however, was a rather narrow and limited opening. Many economies quickly sought to regain their own advantages and set up restrictions as they tried to overcome the consequences of the war and competition in the markets. The global economic crisis greatly exacerbated this tendency. One could speak of a further "internationalization" in the context of the hegemonic politics of National Socialism, albeit in a perverted form: submission in the service of imperial Germanization. True internationalization took place in and with the reconstruction after World War II, primarily under the auspices of Europeanization, but not solely. It was followed by a globalization in the late twentieth century partly characterized by very rapidly expanding but also, partly, no less rapidly retreating movements.

Business owners and companies needed to respond to these challenges. They sought to maintain their survival, further develop their businesses, test new options, and, if possible, focus on long-term sustainability. The specific ways in which the Thyssens went about this, and by means of which they succeeded or failed, are the subject of the studies presented below.

The following observations serve the purpose of presenting, in the necessary brevity, selected results of the corporate-history section. They offer a slice, as it were, of the vast constellation of complex, extensive topics, questions, and information that the authors have compiled from the archives and the literature. They do not aim to be exhaustive but are intended to provide illustrative sources of information and to arouse interest for further reading.

Notes

1. On the period up to the death of August Thyssen and the ongoing effects, see also Wegener, *August and Joseph Thyssen*.
2. August Jr., the second oldest son, and Hedwig, the youngest of the four children, were compensated. On them in detail, see Derix, *Die Thyssens*.
3. E.g., Treue, *Feuer*; Treue and Uebbing, *Feuer*; Eglau, *Fritz Thyssen*; Brakelmann, *Mitschuld*; Litchfield, *Thyssen-Dynastie*.
4. Schanetzky, Review.
5. The name only came into being as a result of a reorganization and renaming in 1971; Gehlen, *Thyssen-Bornemisza-Gruppe*, 11f.
6. See Plumpe, *Unternehmensgeschichte*, 96, 100; Berghoff, *Unternehmensgeschichte*, 42–52. For theoretical and methodological approach, see in detail Wixforth, *Stahlkonzern*, 13–16, 238f.; Gehlen, *Thyssen-Bornemisza-Gruppe*, passim.
7. In his review of Wixforth's Thyssen-Bornemisza study, Karl-Peter Ellerbrock notes that the methodology, which is based on the corporate-governance approach, is "well developed" and "rigorously implemented in the analysis"; *Zeitschrift für Unternehmensgeschichte* 65 (2020), 326f.
8. Diversified business groups are characterized by the presence of dominant owners (often families), tiered ownership across several companies and hierarchical levels, and a heterogeneous product portfolio; cf. Gehlen, *Thyssen-Bornemisza-Gruppe*, 13.
9. See from a comparative perspective Berghoff and Köhler, *Verdienst*, 189–97 et passim.
10. Stiftung Familienunternehmen (ed.), *Volkswirtschaftliche Bedeutung*.
11. Plumpe, *Unternehmensgeschichte*, 86.
12. For the following, see Berghoff, *Unternehmensgeschichte*, 121f.
13. Chandler, *Strategy and Structure*; idem, *Visible Hand*; idem, *Scale and Scope*.
14. Casson, *Entrepreneur*.
15. Discussion and literature on the entrepreneurial typology in Bähr, *Thyssen in der Adenauerzeit*, 91–95; Gehlen, *Thyssen-Bornemisza-Gruppe*, 26–35.
16. Ferguson, *Geschichte der Rothschilds*.
17. Bähr, *Siemens*.
18. Wixforth, *Stahlkonzern*, 192–221; Gehlen, *Thyssen-Bornemisza-Gruppe*, 332ff., 369ff.
19. Derix, *Die Thyssens*, 14–20 et passim.
20. Bähr, *Thyssen in der Adenauerzeit*, 184 et passim.
21. Derix, *Die Thyssens*, 361–78.
22. In detail see Bähr, *Thyssen in der Adenauerzeit*; Hockerts, *Erbe*.
23. From a corporate history perspective, Hartmut Berghoff, "Zähmung des entfesselten Prometheus? Die Generierung von Vertrauenskapital und die Konstruktion des Marktes im Industrialisierungs und Globalisierungsprozess," in Berghoff and Vogel, *Wirtschaftsgeschichte als Kulturgeschichte*, 143–68.
24. See the reflection in Hockerts, *Erbe*, 66f.
25. See in detail Derix, *Die Thyssens*, 369–77 et passim; Gehlen, *Thyssen-Bornemisza-Gruppe*, 59–68.
26. Bähr, *Thyssen in der Adenauerzeit*, 122ff., 181.
27. Ibid., 57–61; see also Schleusener, *Enteignung*, 185; Hockerts, *Erbe*.
28. Details in Bähr, *Thyssen in der Adenauerzeit*, 77, 89, 183.

29. Hockerts, *Erbe*, 75.
30. Lesczenski, *August Thyssen*, 370; Bähr, *Thyssen in der Adenauerzeit*, 160, mentions DM 1.5 billion with reference to a report in *Die Welt* of 5 September 1995. See also the family tree in this volume, 196–97.
31. See Wixforth, *Stahlkonzern*, 232f. with further references.
32. Donges, Urban, Schleusener, and (largely also) Gehlen.
33. Urban, *Zwangsarbeit bei Thyssen*, 25.
34. Gehlen, *Thyssen-Bornemisza-Gruppe*, 230–237; Derix, *Die Thyssens*, 446 ff. et passim.

CHAPTER 4

VEREINIGTE STAHLWERKE AG UNDER NATIONAL SOCIALISM
Corporate Policy between Market Economy and State Economy

(Alexander Donges, 2014)

Donges examines the largest German iron and steel company during the Nazi era, highlighting one of the most important and at the same time most controversial issues of Nazi economic policy: the question of how much room companies had to maneuver under the Nazi dictatorship. Beyond the explicatory interest of the research, the question of corporate responsibility in and for the regime is also always present, either implicitly or explicitly.

The National Socialist economic system is usually characterized as a hybrid of market and state economic elements. In simplified terms: It sought to retain market economy forms and elements under a state command economy. In this context, the National Socialist leaders also intervened in corporate ownership and activities. The Nazi state restricted companies' discretionary rights in a variety of ways, e.g., through state price controls. It moreover contributed to the economic upswing by increasing its own demand, providing subsidies and assuming risks. Further, it confiscated "Jewish" property and that of opponents of the regime. The Nazi state did not establish a state economy, however. As a rule, business property rights were preserved. As Christoph Buchheim and Jonas Scherner—Alexander Donges's scholarly mentors—have pointed out, the regime allowed room for economic rationality. They suggest it provided strong incentives because it considered a profit- and thus incentive-oriented private economy to be more efficient than a coercive economy controlled by command and obedience, especially a state economy.

There was opposition, however, from economic and business historians such as Peter Temin and Peter Hayes. They argued that, at the latest with the second Four-Year Plan in 1936, the National Socialists subjected business owners to their planning will and implemented a kind of cold socialization with massive regulation and the threat of expropriation.[1]

What is beyond dispute is that the National Socialists worked with the help of both incentives and coercion. Controversy centers on the importance or weighting of these two opposing strategies. Did business owners have substantial room to maneuver? If so, how much? In what markets? Under what conditions? To answer these questions, Donges examines the case of Vereinigte Stahlwerke, into which—as explained at the outset—Thyssen had incorporated its heavy industrial companies. He mainly evaluates documents in the ThyssenKrupp Group Archives and the Thyssen Foundation for Industrial History in Duisburg, as well as the records of the Iron and Steel Industry Group in the Federal Archives Berlin and individual records in nine other archives.

Donges builds on the original study by Alfred Reckendrees on the founding and early history of Vereinigte Stahlwerke up to 1933/34.[2] In general, he is concerned with analyzing the entire group for the period from 1933 to 1945. Until now, such an investigation of one of the largest and most important German companies during the Nazi era has been missing. Vestag, formed in 1926 as a merger of several coal and steel companies in the Ruhr region, was a vertically integrated industrial group. It encompassed steel mills and, for the supply of coke, coal mines as well as iron ore and limestone mines, steel and coal trading companies, and shareholdings in the mechanical engineering and processing sectors. Vestag was the largest German steel producer and the second largest in the world, after the American US Steel Corporation. It assumed a key role not only in the German economy of the Nazi era but also in the armaments policy of the National Socialists.

Vestag essentially served as a holding company. Therefore, Donges focuses closely in many places on the respective subsidiaries of the group. Due to the enormous size of the group, the diversity of areas and topics, and the vast source material, it was necessary to limit the selection. Donges thus calls attention to investment policy. As his starting point, he takes Christoph Buchheim's approach to companies' room for maneuver under the Nazi regime. He asks whether and to what extent state actors exerted influence on investment decisions made by corporate management—whether directly or indirectly, whether through coercion or through indirect measures such as regulation.[3]

Donges meticulously examines the corporation's investment policy in areas such as coal mining and final arms production. He concludes that there is no evidence of Vestag investments being made as a result of direct government coercion. In contrast to what had been presented in previous research, even the group's largest investment, the establishment of Gelsenberg-Benzin AG to produce synthetic fuels, was done voluntarily.[4] The group was, moreover, able to implement its own long-term investment strategy, which was complementary to the regime's autarky and armament policy. Donges also manages to rectify earlier research on another important point, namely, the motives of the Nazi state for expropriating the ore fields of the German steel industry and founding the Reichswerke AG für Erzbergbau und Eisenhütten "Hermann Göring" in 1937.

In another case—the sale of Vestag's stake in the Austrian Alpin Montan to the Reichswerke—Donges concludes, conversely, that indirect coercion must have been involved. Ultimately, though, it is a matter of speculation whether the Reich government would have resorted to legal regulation if the company had refused to go along with the deal. He summarizes that "the state itself only became directly engaged in business when its own goals could not be reconciled with the interests of the companies."[5]

Donges makes an additional contribution to the highly complex and controversial issue of indirect corporate control. He interprets the expansion or shift of corporate activities toward armaments and further processing as evasive reactions. The regime subjected the iron and steel market to price regulation, but raw material costs rose there due to the autarky policy. The group accordingly shifted to the manufacture of new or complex products because of the improved margins.

Donges argues emphatically that it "cannot be refuted" that the Vestag investment decisions he studied were due to "the dominance of the profit motive" rather than political pressure. He adds that the group's management made many decisions—such as the start of new work areas like fuel production—that were also dependent on the availability of government subsidies. Under the influence of the armaments directive, Vestag had also set priorities such as the expansion of further processing instead of strengthening the core areas. Donges concludes, however, that Vestag would have acted the same way in the long term "even under a different political regime."[6]

Fritz Thyssen was initially Vestag's second-largest shareholder, after the German Reich. The latter had become the largest investor during the global economic crisis but did not use this to influence corporate decisions. The Reich sold its shares in 1936, which made Fritz Thyssen the largest shareholder. The state would take over his share portfolio after he broke with the Nazi regime, fled, and was expropriated. As before 1936, he had a controlling interest in the group under stock corporation law. But again, this did not translate into any interventions in investment decisions. Things changed during the war; now the Reich exerted influence on the corporation's investment policy, but mainly through its quota policy, not direct investment enforcement.

It becomes apparent that the regime guaranteed private property and entrepreneurial independence if the industrialists demonstrated political loyalty. Donges sees this as a kind of implicit social contract between the regime and German industry. In practice, the state restricted businesses' room for maneuver. In view of the circumstances, it was thought that companies would take the actions the state expected "on their own initiative" whenever possible. Within this context, it was possible for businesses and managers to criticize economic policy measures "without having to fear personal repercussions."[7] If, on the other hand, an entrepreneur took a political stand against the regime, the latter would unleash its full fury—as it did against Fritz Thyssen.

With this joint project, Donges presented the first study on the history of the Vereinigte Stahlwerke under National Socialism. He takes a close look at the well-known broader developments concerning autarky policy, price management, capital market regulation, iron and steel quota systems, and the other regulatory economic interventions. Simultaneously, he examines the group's reactions, objectives, and actions—primarily the economic room for maneuver in investment policy—in a detailed, differentiated, insightful, and comprehensive manner. Frequently, he includes other individual companies and expands the state of research, such as on the Hermann Göring Werke. In this way, he makes a vital contribution to advancing the discussion.

Notes

1. See the account of this controversy with the relevant literature in Donges, *Vereinigte Stahlwerke*, 16–21.
2. Alfred Reckendrees, *Stahltrust*.
3. This is discussed in detail in Donges, *Vereinigte Stahlwerke*, 16ff.
4. Ibid., 176–79.
5. For details, see ibid., 225–87 (quote 286).
6. Ibid., 401–7 (quote 407).
7. Ibid., 402.

CHAPTER 5

FORCED LABOR AT THYSSEN
"Stahlverein" and "Baron-Konzern" in World War II

(Thomas Urban, 2014, 2nd ed. 2021)

It is impossible to contemplate modern corporate history of the Nazi era without considering forced labor. The decision to examine forced labor at Thyssen was a matter of course. Originally, the topic was envisaged to be part of Alexander Donges's study. But it would have gone well beyond the latter's scope. The topic was thus dealt with separately by Thomas Urban.

Among the barely manageable number of Thyssen companies, Urban shortlisted those that were transferred by Fritz Thyssen to the new Vereinigte Stahlwerke AG (Vestag, here: "Stahlverein") or by Heinrich Thyssen-Bornemisza to his new group of companies, August-Thyssen'sche Unternehmungen des In- und Auslande (Atunia, here: "Baron-Konzern"), or in which a member of the entrepreneurial family held a stake either directly or via a holding company.[1] This list had to be further narrowed down due to the inadequate source situation. As a result, the use of forced labor was first investigated in the steel mills belonging to the "Stahlverein" (August Thyssen-Hütte AG) and in the Thyssen plant of Deutsche Röhrenwerke AG Mülheim an der Ruhr. Second, the focus was placed on the two shipyards belonging to the "Baron-Konzern," Bremer Vulkan and Flensburger Schiffsbau-Gesellschaft, and in the coal mine "Gewerkschaft Walsum," located on the left bank of the Rhine near Dinslaken and the most important part of Thyssen'sche Gas und Wasserwerke GmbH.

The main obstacle was the incomplete source material. Urban evaluated materials from around twenty archives and documentation centers. These extended from the ThyssenKrupp corporate archives and the foundation on Thyssen industrial history to municipal archives, chamber of commerce and business archives, state archives, the federal archives, and the Copenhagen state archives, where he viewed important material on recruited Danes. With a detective's instincts, he tracked down previously unexplored material, including material on the "Eastern workers" camp at the Thyssen pipe mill in Mülheim ("Zehntweglager"). Furthermore, in the North Rhine-Westphalia state archive, he discovered the denazification files of two camp leaders, and he found in the Salzgitter AG Group archive affidavits of former camp personnel obtained by the executive board in March 1946, as well as a detailed report of the executive board from 1947 on the "deployment of foreign workers." Such documents are problematic because they were created *ex post facto* under indictment pressure and are apologetic in nature. But it is possible to read them tentatively "against the grain." By combining them with other sources, Urban not only succeeded in providing revealing insights but also offers in his work an approach that stands up to the reservations of historical source criticism.

The term "forced laborers" is known to encompass highly diverse groups: about 8.4 million foreign civilian workers (*Fremdarbeiter*), about 4.6 million prisoners of war, and about 1.7 million prisoners. They were each subject to different legal regimes. Already in the fall of 1941, the Thyssen plant in Mülheim took advantage of the Wehrmacht's initial offer to requisition Soviet prisoners of war to lay tracks for the plant's railroad. The numbers of forced laborers rose rapidly and sharply in all the plants surveyed: in the Mülheim plant, by the fall of 1944, up to 3,455 of the approximately 8,700 workers or about 40 percent of the workforce; most were *Ostarbeiter*, followed by Italians (1 October 1944). At the Vulkan shipyard in Bremen, the proportion was around 25 to 30 percent at the end of 1944 and beginning of 1945. The proportion of foreigners was particularly high at the Walsum mine, a restored or newly founded mine that did not yet have a large core workforce. From 1943 to 1945, they comprised about two-thirds of all workers.[2] These few figures alone show the great importance that forced labor gained in the factories. The question of how information and thus responsibilities were assigned remains difficult to answer. How widespread was knowledge of the fact that forced laborers were used at Thyssen and the circumstances surrounding it? Urban stresses: "In the Thyssen-Bornemisza archival holdings of the foundation for industrial history there are, to the best of our knowledge, no sources available or known about how Heinrich Thyssen-Bornemisza and Wilhelm Roelen [general director of Thyssen'sche Gas und Wasserwerke GmbH and Heinrich Thyssen-Bornemisza's chief representative] stood or behaved regarding the 'deployment of foreigners.'"[3]

Thyssen-Bornemisza commissioned Roelen to "navigate the German-Dutch group of companies through the war period as quietly as possible." The company's top management approved the decision of the "boards of directors of the individual companies to resort to foreign workers, most of whom were recruited under coercion."[4] The boards of directors transferred internal responsibility via the personnel department to the lower level of the company—to master craftsmen, foremen, warehouse supervisors, and guards. These were mostly their own employees but often included retired auxiliary staff, especially in the case of guards.

Urban examines daily camp and work life, food and housing, surveillance, discipline and punishment, the crackdown on "absenteeism," and other areas. He enquires into the room for maneuver of corporate actors under the Nazi regime, utilizing the principal-agent approach wherever possible. By looking at the heterogeneous sources collectively and, if possible, questioning them "against the grain"—i.e., contrary to their original representational intent—he is able to pay particular attention to the level of the "minor perpetrators." This allows for a realistic, three-dimensional, and nuanced picture of the work and life of the forced laborers. Urban vividly describes the typically arduous working and living conditions, especially of Soviet prisoners of war. In the context of the prevailing performance pressure, control, and repression, the actors often had considerable room for maneuver. They could use it for their personal ambition, for distinguishing themselves before superiors, for strengthening their own position within the context of an "elevator effect," for personal enrichment. Alternatively, they could use it for offering help, for being harsh or lenient. There was great latitude, for example, in matters of food, lodging, "reporting" to the Gestapo, and generally in all matters of individual judgment. Declining work performance, for example, could be interpreted as a sign of weakness or illness or as sabotage.

Urban also encountered criminal behavior among the actors as well as escalating violence. With the Mülheim camp leader and his son there were beatings and corruption. The letters from the works council to the management documented from July 1945 onward often contained accusations that a plant manager, foreman, or supervisor had mistreated foreign workers or tolerated assaults.[5] Beyond the recorded cases, there appears to have been a gray area around beatings and mistreatment—albeit less in the plant itself than in the camp. It is striking how often guards moved to other camps of the company, apparently to escape reprisals.

Urban also reveals some surprising details. The fact that the Bremer Vulkan shipyard employed "female Eastern workers" in riveting columns onboard the ships was objected to by the responsible factory inspectorate (it could not be justified "from the point of view of occupational safety," especially during the "cold season"), which made waves all the way to the Reich Ministry of Labor. The latter likewise urged that the employment of female Eastern workers in such "unsuitable work be discontinued." The forced laborers "were disenfranchised and exploited in the barracks camps and factories, deprived of their freedom, their health, and their wages."[6] At the same time, this system of deprivation of liberty, exploitation, and disenfranchisement also included such normative intrusions as the aforementioned intervention of the labor inspectorate.

"Labor deployment" at Thyssen was not fundamentally different from that in other companies. The living and working conditions of forced laborers were generally not significantly better or worse than elsewhere. Differences mostly resulted from peculiarities of the respective companies. In summarizing, Urban arrives at the verdict: "There is accordingly nothing unique to Thyssen."[7]

How the plant managers as "principals" reacted to misconduct by their "agents" is very rarely documented. Many things were settled verbally. Looking the other way and leniency were apparently common, but there were also reassignments, fines, and, in extreme cases, dismissal. After the war, many things came to light during the denazification proceedings that had previously been hidden. Here, too, leniency for the perpetrators was widespread. This partly occurred in the context of mutual exoneration of employees and supervisors, but also in the context of British occupation policy. Most of the plants studied here were in fact located in the British zone. For the British, it was important to get the economy going again as soon as possible.

In August 1945, the new chairman of August Thyssen-Hütte AG, Eduard Herzog, had "guidelines for the political purging of the operations" drawn up. They stipulated punishments for "political offenses," informing on others during the Nazi era, and for continuing adherence to National Socialism. The physical punishment of prisoners or foreign workers—provided it did not take "brutal forms"—was expressly not described to be so serious that it warranted dismissal, reassignment, or similar disciplinary action. Rather, "it should be recognized that supervisory staff often had a difficult position during the war, on the one hand, with regard to the often-challenging behavior of prisoners of war and foreign workers, and, on the other hand, with regard to the demands of factory management to fulfill certain required services with the prisoners."[8] These guidelines also aimed to get operations back to the start of production as soon as possible. The guidelines, Urban emphasizes, were "groundbreaking for dealing with the issue of forced labor in the context of denazification." By issuing exculpatory rulings, many committees helped "minor offenders" to reenter the workforce under new political circumstances.[9]

From all we know, the fact that the executive boards of both Thyssen and Thyssen-Bornemisza utilized forced laborers was due to the functional logic of ensuring production and survival in the wartime economic system. Not only had civilian production lost importance, but Thyssen's plants were also integrated into armaments and war production. Part of this logic was to fill the gaps and bottlenecks caused by military conscription with civilian workers, prisoners of war from the East, and other forces, and to try meet the ever-increasing demands of war production with whatever manpower was available. Forced labor was considered necessary, and the regime encouraged its use—most emphatically in the case of production backlogs. Urban points out that after the Reich had secured Fritz Thyssen's shares following his escape, the corporate boards were careful not to provoke (further) conflict by refusing to cooperate or by appearing insufficiently committed to the regime and the war economy's requirements. Indeed, there are no known cases of expropriation on this account. But based on experience, the regime would have resorted to personnel consequences and replaced senior executives. Still, as Urban underlines, this does not absolve them of responsibility for using forced labor.

When comparing Heinrich Thyssen-Bornemisza with other entrepreneurs during the Nazi era, it becomes clear that he was neither aggressively geared toward business expansion or close cooperation with the Nazi regime, as was the case with Friedrich Flick, nor did he seek to create safe havens or barriers within the company in the face of National Socialism, as was the case with Paul Reusch (Gutehoffnungshütte). The aim was for his companies to "get by" (*durchkommen*); he avoided confrontation. But this, of course, does not relieve him of his share of the responsibility.[10]

In terms of their type, the leading managers in the companies studied here were rational, career-oriented, technician-entrepreneurs or managers with a great propensity to adapt. Some of the Thyssen directors were members of the NSDAP; none held an office there. All of them, however, came to terms with the Nazi state and the wartime economic conditions. They sought to leverage the latter for positioning and the further development of their plants. Roelen, for example, took advantage of the growing demand for coal to expand the Walsum mine. As mentioned, production there was carried out to a considerable extent by requisitioned Soviet forced laborers. These workers were assigned against their will, suffered "under inhumane conditions," and many of them died. The Thyssen managers allegedly were concerned with getting the greatest possible performance out of the forced laborers. In this respect, they were no different from operations managers in other companies. They had considerable latitude for demonstrating either harshness or leniency; they exercised both for exacting severe punishments and exhibiting generosity. Regarding individual problems or conflicts, the maxim prevailed that the course of operations should not be impeded.

After 1945, Roelen, like Robert Kabelac, director of the Bremen Vulkan shipyard, was able to maintain his executive post.[11] After the war, the Allies assigned only one of the Thyssen directors studied here to an internment camp. This was Fritz Winterhoff, the manager of the Thyssen pipe mill, where the conditions in the "Russian camp" in Mülheim on Zehntweg had been particularly grim. He died in 1946 before he could be tried.[12]

Urban's study combines insights into the day-to-day lives of forced laborers with an account of the general business and political contexts. It thus complements the corporate history of Vestag by Donges, which is oriented toward economic reasoning. Urban's study, whose second edition has been recently published, has received much critical acclaim.[13]

Notes

1. Urban, *Zwangsarbeit*, 24f.
2. As of 1 October 1944; ibid., 63, 84, 101.
3. Ibid., 45.
4. Ibid., 165.
5. Ibid., 146.
6. Ibid., 165.
7. Ibid., 163.
8. Guidelines from August 1945, quoted here from ibid., 145f.
9. Ibid., 171.
10. Emphatically ibid., 165.
11. Ibid., 166ff.
12. Ibid., 29f., 166f.
13. Jens Binner in his review for *H-Soz-Kult* 15 July 2016: "carefully crafted study," "rewarding," "fruitful"; Matthias Gomoll in his review in *ZUG* 61 (2016): 238f.: Urban offers "an exciting look into the subject matter."

CHAPTER 6

THE EXPROPRIATION OF FRITZ THYSSEN
Dispossession and Restitution

(Jan Schleusener, 2018)

In the second third of the twentieth century, the "case" of Fritz Thyssen[1] stands out historically. His associations with the Nazi regime and the consequences he faced are characterized by four aspects that are rather unusual in their combination.

First: He was an early supporter of the National Socialist "movement." Fritz Thyssen was an exponent of heavy industry and was arrested in the revolution after World War I. He was stylized a "national hero" in 1923 in the "Ruhrkampf" because he had defied French orders in the context of reparations and had been convicted. He was a Catholic and monarchist with corporatist ideas. An early supporter of Hitler, he hoped that the National Socialists would restore his pre-1918 world, which had fallen into disarray, and, in particular, restore patriarchal leadership to industry. He was courted by the National Socialists but not taken seriously. His alienation with NS actors began soon after 1933. He failed to find acceptance for his ideas and was outraged by attacks on institutions of the Catholic Church and the discrimination and persecution of Jews. Ardent anticommunist that he was, he saw the Hitler-Stalin Pact of 24 August 1939 as a betrayal by Hitler of National Socialist aims. He canceled his participation in a Reichstag session on 1 September 1939 and hastily fled with his wife to Switzerland, breaking with Hitler and Nazi politics.

Second: He went into exile and was expropriated. The Nazi regime saw it as a loss of prestige that this former model industrialist had broken away from it and attacked Hitler.[2] It wanted to keep the case quiet and offered Thyssen the chance to return unmolested to Germany. Thyssen declined. He was promptly expatriated, and his assets—which the Reich Security Main Office estimated at 270 million Reichsmarks in 1940—were confiscated. The expropriation of a non-Jewish entrepreneur under National Socialism was highly unusual. It was done quickly for the benefit of the Prussian state. The latter reacted more quickly than the authorities of the Reich; Hermann Göring's interests as Prussian prime minister and commissioner for the Four-Year Plan evidently played a role here. Thyssen had cultivated friendly relations with him. Fritz and Amélie Thyssen went to France to flee from there to Argentina but ended up in Nazi custody.

Third: He was a Nazi prisoner. The couple were imprisoned in a sanatorium and then in concentration camps; they survived the war under perilous circumstances. The end of the war did not bring Thyssen his liberation. In France, together with the American journalist Emery Reves, he had begun to work on a book about his relationship with National Socialism and started a media offensive against the Nazi regime. Both came to a halt with the German invasion of Paris. Reves lost contact with Thyssen. In 1941, after the *London Times* reported that Thyssen had died in a concentration camp, Reves published a book under Thyssen's name with the clever marketing title *I Paid Hitler*. Since then, Thyssen has been regarded, above all in the United States, as a major financier of the National Socialists. He learned about the

Figure 6.1. Adolf Hitler with Fritz Thyssen (behind Hitler, right), Albert Vögler (Vereinigte Stahlwerke AG), and Walter Borbet (Bochumer Verein) during a plant tour in the Ruhr region on 8 April 1936. Photo: Heinrich Hoffmann.

publication only after the end of the war. He always denied writing the book, but it turned out to be a heavy burden for him.[3] The Americans imprisoned him as a supporter of Hitler.

Fourth: His was denazified despite also being persecuted. He had assumed that he had effectively denazified himself given his fate between 1940 and 1945. The Americans' imprisonment of him left him embittered. It was unusual that a person persecuted by the Nazi regime and an inmate of a concentration camp had to undergo denazification proceedings after the war. He was at once a defendant and a recipient of restitution. In his denazification proceedings in Königstein, Hesse, he was represented by the Cologne lawyer Robert Ellscheid. His sister-in-law had recommended him as legal counsel in 1945, and he had been his advisor and trustee ever since.[4]

The responsible *Spruchkammer* (German civilian court handling denazification) was faced with a difficult task: how could the person concerned be classified into one of the four groups prescribed by law—principal culprits, incriminated, lesser incriminated, fellow travelers—when none of these categories adequately captured such a varied past with National Socialism? Schleusener finds that the court proceeded equitably.[5] It explored the question—which went far beyond this case—of whether one could make up for earlier guilt through later resistance to the regime. It concluded that this was possible only if one had done more harm to the Nazi state through one's later behavior than one had benefited from its earlier support. The court rejected this argument here: Thyssen had by no means fully exhausted his opportunities to support the opposition and resistance. The *Spruchkammer* classified him as a "lesser offender" (*Minderbelasteter*) and imposed a property penalty of 15 percent and a lump sum of 7.5 percent of his registered assets in Germany; the latter was subsequently greatly diminished. Fritz Thyssen did not file an appeal. He had now been in prison for almost ten years and wanted to go to Argentina. Sick and resentful, he emigrated and died in Argentina in 1951.

Apart from the denazification process, a fierce struggle began for the restitution of business and private assets. At first, it was blocked by the Allies. Later, after the foundation of the Federal Republic, the German authorities feared, Thyssen might sell his businesses to Belgium, and that would lead to a sell-off of industry in the Ruhr. The disputes over restitutions lasted until shortly before Thyssen's death, and the settlement process lasted even longer. In this study, Johannes Bähr looks at the development of Fritz Thyssen's companies after the war.

Schleusener explored the subject at the forefront of research with the help of unprinted sources from about a dozen archives in Germany, America, Great Britain, and Switzerland. While he deals only briefly with what was already known, he centers on the years after 1939, where he considerably expands the state of research. Schleusener goes beyond property law issues in the narrower sense and examines the motives for Thyssen's support of National Socialism. The importance of Amélie Thyssen is also brought to the fore. Like her husband, she had been an early supporter of National Socialism. She went through thick and thin with him, even during his escape and imprisonment, and was a tremendous help in compensating for his fickle, capricious, and at times impulsive behavior. Her support is particularly evident during his *Spruchkammer* proceedings—one of the few times they were apart and largely left to their own devices.

Schleusener reveals that Fritz Thyssen's expropriation also had consequences for his cousins Hans and Julius Thyssen, the sons of Joseph, a brother of August Thyssen. Since the Prussian state wanted to take full control of the holding company after the confiscation, it bought the brothers' shares—in part with funds that had accrued to it "since November 1938 through the Jewish property levy, which from the standpoint of property rights seems noteworthy."[6] It is likewise interesting that Prussia had relied on the "Law on the Confiscation of Communist Property" (of 26 May 1933) in expropriating the anticommunist Fritz Thyssen.

Other important findings in Schleusener's work can only be touched on here. These include the fact that after the invasion of the Netherlands the Germans discovered Thyssen assets and proceeded to impose back taxes and confiscate assets to the detriment of Fritz, Hans, and Julius Thyssen.[7] Furthermore, there was a bizarre dispute between the states of Hesse, North Rhine-Westphalia and the federal government over who was responsible for restitution of Thyssen assets confiscated in 1939 in favor of Prussia after Prussia had ceased to exist.[8] Finally, in another lucky find, Schleusener details the tough, bitter dispute that took place mainly from 1953 to 1955 between the Thyssen lawyers and those of Robert Bosch GmbH. Ostensibly, it involved securities from Fritz Thyssen's confiscated assets, which the Nazi trustee had sold to Robert Bosch. Bosch and Thyssen had died in 1942 and 1951, respectively. The case now concerned the behavior of two politically diametrically opposed industrialists under National Socialism.[9]

Fritz Thyssen paid a high price for his support of National Socialism. He was, as Schleusener remarks, "not so much a National Socialist as an authoritarian nationalist and anti-Bolshevik." In the words of the author, Fritz Thyssen "was the only Reichstag member who openly protested against the unleashing of war, and he was the only major industrialist to declare war on the Nazi regime." He thus holds "unique standing not only in the economic but also in the political history of the Nazi era."[10]

Notes

1. For the following, unless otherwise noted, see Eglau, *Fritz Thyssen*; Schleusener, *Enteignung*.
2. Schleusener, *Enteignung*, 12; on the press response, see, in detail, de Taillez, *Bürgerleben*, 414–23.
3. For details on *I Paid Hitler*, see de Taillez, *Bürgerleben*, 423–44, 484. See also Schleusener, Enteignung, 11f.
4. Bähr, *Thyssen in der Adenauerzeit*, 54–56; Schleusener, *Enteignung*, 146f.
5. Ibid., 239.
6. Ibid., 208–12, 237 (quote).
7. See, in detail, ibid., pp. 121–31, 237.
8. For more details, see ibid., 179–212.
9. In detail, ibid., 225–34.
10. Ibid., 236, 241.

CHAPTER 7

THYSSEN IN THE ADENAUER ERA
Corporate Formation and Family Capitalism

(Johannes Bähr, 2015)

Johannes Bähr describes the reemergence and expansion of August Thyssen-Hütte (ATH) after the Allied demerger of Vereinigte Stahlwerke in the three decades following the end of the war. After the confiscation in 1939, the company became a family business again; yet by the end of the 1960s, it lost this character once and for all. Bähr deals in sequence with the dismantling and demerger of Vereinigte Stahlwerke, the efforts to reestablish a new family business, the rise of the new August Thyssen-Hütte to become one of the biggest German and European steel producers, and, finally, the transformation from family business to publicly owned corporation. Since he could only draw on a limited body of research, he evaluated many unprinted sources from some fifteen archives in Germany and abroad, including new information on the South American family estate of Amélie and Fritz's daughter Anita Countess Zichy-Thyssen.[1] His study is a slice of West German economic history that links several fields of action and could not be more concise. Furthermore, it impressively depicts the systematic intertwining of family and business history.

The first dimension is that of the ever-changing business development of Germany's most important steel group alongside Krupp—from integration to de-integration and re-integration, which was partly a new integration. In 1926, the Thyssens had transferred most of the heavy industrial activities of their family group to Vereinigte Stahlwerke AG, thus completing a corporate integration. After World War II, the Allied occupying powers reversed this as part of their demerger policy, thereby creating about a dozen and a half independent successor companies. Thyssen's share in Vestag was 20.74 percent; he then had an equivalent share in the successor companies, but with divestment requirements. As a result, the Thyssens became major shareholders in six successor companies. Amélie Thyssen's shareholdings were consolidated by Fritz Thyssen Vermögensverwaltung AG, Cologne, and those of Anita Gräfin Zichy-Thyssen by Thyssen AG für Beteiligungen,

Düsseldorf. While it is not possible to go into the details here,[2] the two main steps can be mentioned. In 1955, following internal power struggles, several share swaps and difficult and protracted negotiations involving not only the German government but also initially the Allies and then the High Authority of the European Coal and Steel Community in Luxembourg, Thyssen's successor companies Hüttenwerke Phoenix AG and Rheinische Röhrenwerke AG (Rheinrohr) merged to form Phoenix-Rheinrohr AG Vereinigte Hütten und Röhrenwerk. This next merged in 1963/64 with August Thyssen-Hütte (ATH), also a successor company to Vestag. The two heirs were also major shareholders in ATH. They had already increased their share in the company to 52.9 percent in 1956 by means of a share swap and an increase in capital. With this and other successor companies to Vestag, Amélie Thyssen had ensured that the Thyssen group once again became a family business in the sense of a family-owned firm (Mark Casson). This was some thirty years after Fritz Thyssen had transferred his industrial holdings to Vestag.

But this did not last long. The company—already Europe's second-largest steel producer in the mid-1960s—continued to expand, partly through the acquisition of Mannesmann's steel operations in 1969/70 and Rheinische Stahlwerke in 1973. The Thyssen group had a share of around 30 percent of German steel production in the mid-1970s. In the face of European and global competition, the need for capital increased so much that the family could no longer keep up. Soon after Amélie Thyssen's death in August 1965, the capital stock grew to such an extent that Thyssen'sche Vermögensverwaltung and the Fritz Thyssen Stiftung together no longer held a majority stake in August Thyssen-Hütte. As the company's capital requirements continued to grow, the family's share gradually fell to around a quarter of the share capital. After a few years as a family business, ATH at last had become a publicly owned corporation.

The second dimension is the political one in the narrower sense. For companies of this size, proximity to politics and power is crucial for the day-to-day business, currying favor, and establishing favorable political contacts and connections. Many authors consider close relations with the state and its authorities to be characteristic of the German model of cooperative, corporatist capitalism.[3] Of course, as Fritz Thyssen's fate shows, this could also be dangerous. For Thyssen's corporate development in the postwar period, the backing of the federal government in the German as well as in the European context was of major importance in several respects. For one thing, it meant economic support of the company's rebuilding by the federal government and North Rhine-Westphalia, where most of the plants were located. Without financial support from the public sector, even the initial reconstruction phase of the August Thyssen-Hütte, which was badly damaged in the war, would not have been possible. The construction of a hot strip mill would likewise have not occurred without political support.⁴ This technological leap dramatically advanced ATH and gave it an invaluable advantage over its competitors. The connections of Robert Pferdmenges, one of the few personal friends of the chancellor, and the Thyssen family's contacts with Konrad Adenauer, which stretched back to his time as mayor of Cologne, were instrumental in financing the investments and securing business decisions in the political arena.

These contacts intensified and strengthened when Adenauer managed to stop the dismantlements at the end of 1949. It was his first major success as chancellor. He received enormous gratitude and recognition for it from the ATH Works council chairman and DGB chairman Hans Böckler, which strengthened his position vis-à-vis the SPD. Bähr estimates that by then "a special relationship had developed between the government leader" and ATH. Sohl, the chairman of the board, repeatedly took advantage of the group's high-level connections, especially with Adenauer, whom he induced to bring his ideas to the attention of U.S. high commissioner John J. McCloy.⁵ Amélie Thyssen maintained a close relationship with Adenauer until her death. When she and her daughter established the Fritz Thyssen Foundation and contributed a large block of shares as endowment capital, Adenauer personally awarded her the Grand Cross of the Order of Merit of the Federal Republic of Germany at her Puchhof estate near Straubing in 1960. Her daughter Anita received the Grand Cross of Merit with Star in Argentina from the German ambassador.⁶

Political support was also important at the European level. The merger of Phoenix-Rheinrohr AG with August Thyssen-Hütte was subject to the approval of the High Authority of the European Coal and Steel Community. The merger was a key event for Thyssen in the reconstruction process. As mentioned above, both companies had emerged from the demerger of Vereinigte Stahlwerke. There was no prohibition on acquisitions, thus leaving open the option of forming a group later. If one takes as a yardstick that Thyssen's asset management companies held most of the share capital in both companies, Phoenix-Rheinrohr had been a Thyssen family company since its foundation in 1955, ATH since at least mid-1956.⁷ The supervisory board chairmen were Pferdmenges (ATH) and Ellscheid (Phoenix-Rheinrohr). Amélie saw it as obligation to her husband's legacy to rebuild a Thyssen family corporation. Her daughter, by contrast, was primarily interested in the highest possible dividends for herself and her two sons. She had moved to Argentina in 1940 and transferred her parents' assets in Switzerland, which had been signed over to her. After her divorce in 1946, she and her asset manager and new partner Baron Guillermo von Winterhalder made costly investments, especially in agriculture—not for the purpose of international diversification but as a capital investment. These ventures certainly incurred heavy losses.

She and her sons, moreover, enjoyed very lavish lifestyles. Baron Winterhalder repeatedly tried to transfer parts of their assets to Argentina. Kurt Birrenbach, their German asset manager, was always concerned about the stability of their German industrial holdings. Winterhalder died in 1967. Amélie moved to Germany in 1974. Her sons were successful in Argentina in agriculture (cattle farming) and as large landowners.[8] Ellscheid, who was also chairman of the supervisory board of Fritz Thyssen Vermögensverwaltung, Cologne, which managed Amélie's investments, wanted to secure the highest possible returns for the two women. The driving force behind the merger proposal, ATH CEO Hans-Günther Sohl, sought expansion of ATH and the top management position in the newly formed corporation.[9] After a complicated prelude,[10] Sohl finally submitted the application for approval of the merger of the two companies on 29 October 1958. The proposal was well prepared, and Adenauer personally lobbied for it. But the Luxembourg authorities caused trouble, threatening to impose significant conditions. The reason was fears in France and other countries of a resurgence of the once powerful Vereinigte Stahlwerke—which, however, were more politically than economically motivated. Sohl finally had to withdraw the proposal on 27 April 1960. A subsequent attempt in May 1963 proved successful. Above and beyond the elimination of antitrust concerns, the political reconciliation between Germany and France was instrumental. Before this, it was hardly conceivable that the French president General de Gaulle would pay a visit to a German steel company, August Thyssen-Hütte, during his 1962 visit to Germany and praise the achievements in the Ruhr to the applause of around four thousand Thyssen workers.[11]

While such business and political dimensions were quite apparent to contemporaries, the same cannot be said for the constellations behind them. The actors' motives and their decision-making and negotiation processes remained obscure. A circle of advisors operated at this level. The most important—the "Thyssen committee"[12]—consisted of four individuals: One was the banker Robert Pferdmenges, an old friend of the Thyssen family with very good access to the capital market and excellent contacts in politics; he was a member of the Bundestag and a friend of Konrad Adenauer. Another was the Cologne lawyer Robert Ellscheid. He had been referred to Fritz Thyssen by his sister-in-law. Ellscheid successfully defended him in the *Spruchkammer* proceedings, was appointed his attorney and executor, and was the widow's general agent. The third member of the circle was Kurt Birrenbach, lawyer, politician, and general agent of Thyssen's daughter Anita Zichy-Thyssen. The fourth, who joined during the consultations on the new integration, was Hans-Günther Sohl, chairman of the executive board of August Thyssen-Hütte from 1953 to 1973, previously a member of the executive board of Vereinigte Stahlwerke (from 1941, then again from 1947) and re-

Figure 7.1. French president Charles de Gaulle addresses the workforce of August Thyssen-Hütte AG during his visit to Germany on 6 September 1962. Photo: Günter Meyer, works photographer at August Thyssen-Hütte AG.

sponsible for its demerger. He was later a skilled and power-conscious president of the Federation of German Industries (1972-76).[13]

With political support and economic good fortune, ATH became the center of the new Thyssenkonzern instead of Phoenix-Rheinrohr. This occurred even though the prerequisites and many plans had tended to favor Rheinrohr. ATH was in a worse starting position after 1945 compared to Phoenix-Rheinrohr. Among other things, it was smaller and more heavily damaged. ATH, however, was ultimately the more successful branch. But why?[14]

First, the hard-charging ATH boss Sohl acted more skillfully and with greater success than his counterpart at Rheinrohr, Fritz-Aurel Goergen. Sohl prevailed over Ellscheid, who was chairman of the supervisory board of Phoenix-Rheinrohr and had engineered the merger of the two predecessor companies. What's more, Sohl was able to secure the support of Pferdmenges, senior politicians, and, especially, Amélie. In the end, Goergen was overthrown. Second, ATH was able to beat Rheinrohr in the race to build the hot strip mill. This, again, was the cornerstone of the company's great economic success. Here, the focus was on the right future trend: on flat steel instead of semifinished products, steel girders, and railroad rails, which were important for the railroads and heavy industry. Flat steel was needed to meet the rapidly growing demand from the automotive, electrical, and mechanical engineering industries.

The new plant became a powerful symbol of the reconstruction, Thyssens' resurgence, and the German "economic miracle." At the festive launch on 11 July 1955 (followed by an official ceremony), Amélie Thyssen was joined by top representatives from politics and business at the August Thyssen iron and steel mill in Duisburg-Hamborn—including Konrad Adenauer, German economics minister Ludwig Erhard, German interior minister Gerhard Schröder and North Rhine-Westphalian minister president Karl Arnold. Sohl cleverly took advantage of the festivities to set the stage: the occasion signified an overcoming of the dismantlements, renewal and rebuilding, and, finally, Thyssen's resurgence.

The Thyssen committee was not involved in day-to-day operations. The circle of advisors was central to fundamental business issues, like a "board of trustees" in the literal sense of the term. Decisions and strategic moves were deliberated, prepared, and, as a rule, implemented. Each of the four had his own area of responsibility, which the others respected. The discussions were frequently contentious and hot-tempered. From the start of 1958, there was a minute taker. It was clear to all involved that the decision-making power lay with the two female shareholders. The fact that this model worked, proved effective and sustainable, was primarily due to the trust that Amélie Thyssen placed in the four grand seigneurs. She was able to draw on many years of experience and was open to advice. The model also succeeded because the cooperation continued despite different points of view and disagreements. It also depended on the skill to involve and win over the shareholders. The manner and extent to which they did this is another significant factor in their success: they exhibited an ability for sustained diplomacy, tact, attention to detail, and a willingness to pay court, as well as to take on day-to-day services, do extra work, etc., all without completely denying their own self-interests.[15] Bähr illustrates the power structures behind such a cooperation using the toppling of Goergen as an example. Not only was the latter economically successful, but he apparently was also backed by members of the board. Nevertheless, he acted clumsily and arrogantly; he also bruised egos, including that of Amélie Thyssen. Besides this, he also stood in Sohl's way. Bähr's conclusion: "Goergen's fall is vivid proof that the rules of a family-owned firm applied at Phoenix-Rheinrohr. At the end of the day, one of the most successful Ruhr industrialists and prominent managers in the country could be dismissed by an almost eighty-year-old widow because she was the majority stakeholder." Goergen was finally generously compensated.[16]

Notes

1. Bähr, *Thyssen in der Adenauerzeit*, 161–67. On this topic, see also Hockerts, *Erbe*, 71–77, 204f.
2. On the processes described here, see ibid., 66–91; Hockerts, *Erbe*, 80–93.
3. See, for example, Berghoff, *Unternehmensgeschichte*, 96, 185ff.
4. For more details, see Bähr, *Thyssen in der Adenauerzeit*, 37ff. For example, Sohl enlisted the help of Robert Pferdmenges as well as the chancellor and several federal ministers to ensure that ATH, rather than other interested parties such as Hüttenwerke Ruhrort-Meiderich under its CEO Fritz-Aurel Goergen, could build the hot strip mill. The plant gave ATH an outstanding competitive advantage. See ibid., 38f.
5. This is discussed in detail in ibid., 32, 34 (quotes).
6. The Fritz Thyssen Foundation received from Amélie Thyssen DM 74.7 million nominal shares and from Anita DM 25.3 million nominal shares in ATH. The share price was 203 percent of the nominal value, i.e., the market value was DM 203 million; ibid., 150ff.; on this subject in detail, see Hockerts, *Erbe*, 116f.
7. Bähr, *Thyssen in der Adenauerzeit*, 72, 93ff. Thyssen'sche Vermögensverwaltungen held 50.38 percent of ATH share capital in July 1956, 37.19 percent in July 1959, 35.78 percent in July 1969; see the overviews, ibid., 89, 152.
8. Bähr, *Thyssen in der Adenauerzeit*, 161–67; Hockerts, *Erbe*, 71–77, 204f.
9. Ibid., 73; Hockerts, *Erbe*, 13, 45–70.
10. See in detail Bähr, *Thyssen in der Adenauerzeit*, 72–91; Hockerts, *Erbe*, 121f.
11. Bähr, *Thyssen in der Adenauerzeit*, 145ff.; Hockerts, *Erbe*, 122.
12. Bähr, *Thyssen in der Adenauerzeit*, 54ff., 73ff., 101ff.; Hockerts, *Erbe*, 47–70, 82, with new source findings.
13. Bähr, *Thyssen in der Adenauerzeit*, 22f.; Hockerts, *Erbe*, 13, 56f. et passim; Berghahn, *Sohl*.
14. On this and the following, see Bähr, *Thyssen in der Adenauerzeit*, 111–25; Hockerts, *Erbe*, 83–86, 120f.
15. Bähr, *Thyssen in der Adenauerzeit*, 91–110; Hockerts, *Erbe*, 45–70. Based on new source findings, Hockerts is better able to estimate the seriousness of the internal dispute within the committee than Bähr, 81.
16. With DM 2.6 million. Quote and details in Bähr, ibid., 97ff. Amélie Thyssen admittedly acted on the advice of Pferdmenges, which sheds light on his influence.

CHAPTER 8

FROM STEEL GROUP TO CORPORATE GROUP
The Heinrich Thyssen-Bornemisza Companies from 1926–1932

(Harald Wixforth, 2019)

Until now, as discussed above, the "Thyssen" name has mainly been associated with Thyssen AG and its predecessors—in short, the heavy industrial division of August or Fritz Thyssen. It is not widely known that an internationally successful conglomerate also emerged from the founder's legacy. How did Heinrich Thyssen-Bornemisza manage to organize, lead, and successfully steer his heterogeneous inheritance through the Great Depression and subsequent crises and catastrophes? Harald Wixforth examines this question, drawing on records in company and state archives for the period from the formation of the "Baron-Konzern" to Heinrich Thyssen-Bornemisza's move to Switzerland in 1932. From that point on, Heinrich increasingly devoted himself to his interests as an art collector.

Heinrich Thyssen-Bornemisza fled with his family from Hungary to the Netherlands in 1919. He then became involved in his father's Dutch companies, especially in banking, transportation, and logistics. His focus became the Bank voor Handel en Scheepvaart (BHS) in Rotterdam, founded there in 1918 by Thyssen's N.V. Handels- en Transport Maatschapij Vulcaan for the coal and ore trade. It was obviously also set up to secure and conceal Thyssen's capital commitments and asset holdings. The bank became the financial center of Thyssen's ventures in the Netherlands, Germany, and beyond. In 1920, Vulcaan established a shipping company in Rotterdam for ocean shipping, Halcoyn-Lijn, N. V., and its own port, Havenbedrijf "Vlaardingen-Oost" N. V.[1] Thyssen-Bornemisza's business interests lay in commerce, especially banking.

Beyond the company units he contributed to Vereinigte Stahlwerke, Heinrich Thyssen-Bornemisza had inherited a heterogeneous conglomerate. The emphasis was on Dutch (coal) trading companies, shipping companies and shipyards, metal processing, the energy industry, and the building materials industry. Ownership relations were unusually convoluted and intertwined. Fritz and his two cousins Hans and Julius Thyssen initially continued to hold shares in the companies Heinrich inherited, and vice versa. As mentioned above, Heinrich did not become the sole owner of the company until 1936. Moreover, several of the stock corporations also had outside shareholders who held minority stakes.[2]

How does one organize, manage, and control such a heterogeneous entity? Thyssen-Bornemisza took up his father's ideas of setting up a general management board for the group under the family's controlling influence. He combined his companies in the relatively new form of a holding company, which had come from America and was only gradually becoming widespread in Germany. In 1927, August Thyssen'sche Unternehmungen des In und Auslandes GmbH (Atunia) was founded with headquarters in Düsseldorf. It was headed by a board of directors as a management and control body, which included the directors of the most important group companies. Heinrich Thyssen-Bornemisza was chair and had decision-making power. The companies remained independent and were run by their directors. The board served the purpose of coordination. As there was no control or profit transfer agreement, it constituted a "loose merger."[3]

This body, however, was of little significance. While Thyssen-Bornemisza initially frequently attended meetings, he became "increasingly passive"—even on pivotal issues—and conceded "autonomy more and more to his plant directors and legal advisors." As time passed, other, more effective instruments of control and management clearly gained the upper hand—indirect management, control with the help of operational performance indicators—and superseded Heinrich's involvement in the board of directors' meetings. By 1932, the board of directors no longer had a coordinating function.[4]

Beyond the coordination of the individual companies in Atunia, Heinrich Thyssen-Bornemisza aimed at the asset coordination and control of the group and its property. At the end of 1926, soon after the inheritance, he established the Kaszony Family Foundation in the Swiss canton of Schwyz in the village of the same name, with 100,000 francs in initial capital. Its purpose was to "support the family members and secure and maintain the inherited family assets." Heinrich Thyssen-Bornemisza was the founder and, during his lifetime, only member of the foundation's board of trustees. He was thus the sole decision-maker. By 1932, he had transferred most of his industrial holdings to the Kaszony Family Foundation and placed them under its management. The foundation became what was arguably Thyssen-Bornemisza's most important instrument for transferring assets to safe, neutral, and discreet Switzerland and for managing his corporate group.

It served as a hub for transfers between individual companies across national borders and for the tax-saving, tax-avoiding, and not infrequently tax-evading handling of profits.[5]

As Boris Gehlen has revealed, Heinrich Thyssen-Bornemisza combined all this with an ingenious system for measuring efficiency and thus also for controlling his individual companies. He did so by cooperating with another company in the group: Rotterdamsch Trustee's Kantoor (RTK), a kind of public accounting firm. RTK provided the business owner with the key figures of his individual companies—which he needed to assess efficiency, profitability, and profit, and thus use as a basis for strategic decision-making in his corporate realm. RTK was responsible for the administration of the Kaszony Foundation. Taken together, they were the linchpin to a complicated and, from the outside, rather opaque transnational scheme of asset protection and corporate governance. They were a veritable depot for marshaling assets and useful for responding to political, fiscal, and economic incentives and challenges. Both German authorities during the Nazi era and American authorities during the occupation attempted to penetrate the corporate web and financial transactions, but with little success.[6]

After August Thyssen's death, his son Heinrich initially became heavily involved in the company's daily management. He frequently attended meetings of the Atunia board of directors, was briefed, and participated in certain discussions. But his interest soon waned—he was less on hand and liked to leave decisions to the directors, a propensity he had exhibited previously. He often intervened only when there was disagreement among the managers. As a result, Thyssen's ventures could not be controlled centrally by means of Atunia's board of directors or from this body. On the one hand, the will and self-interest of the plant directors were too strong. On the other, Heinrich Thyssen-Bornemisza's own readiness—and apparently also his ability—to intervene and decide in a mediatory, conciliatory manner and, if necessary, through his own authority was too feeble. Two reasons for this seem to have been the nature and aptitudes of the company's leader, along with his increasing awareness of the information asymmetries between his directors and himself.

While the owner's reluctance increased the directors' room for maneuver, the internal potential for conflict grew. If it had been assumed that the individual companies in the network would preferentially help each other, it soon became apparent that the self-assured managers of the Thyssen-Bornemisza companies were concluding contracts with third parties when this was more beneficial to them. The Bank voor Handel en Scheepvaart in particular, under its enterprising head Hendrik Jozef Kouwenhoven, not only served as the holding companies' house bank but also increasingly cooperated with other companies.[7]

The success of the "Baron-Konzern" resulted less from the direct intervention of the company owner than from the fact that the group companies were run by managers who were highly qualified, energetic, competent, and, finally, loyal. In addition, they acted in an independent manner with a view to profitability. The importance of managers for Thyssen-Bornemisza is shown, among other things, by the fact that his decision to focus his activities on the gas business resulted from more than the business area's growing economic importance. In Franz Lenze, whom he retained from his father, he also had an esteemed expert for the field. Lenze died in an accident in 1937.[8] The plant directors were mostly in-house talent: professionally socialized, promoted, and molded at Thyssen. Heinrich Thyssen-Bornemisza took advantage of the continuing influence and tradition of his plant managers from their work under August Thyssen and held on to them. He offered incentives—since he generally respected the managers' room for maneuver and discretionary power[9]—and attractive remuneration, which usually also included a strong performance component.[10]

The new holding company faced major challenges. Following the currency reform of 1923, great financial difficulties were caused by the stabilization crisis. In addition, the operations of the group had to be realigned. The aim was to make up for the loss of business relations with the companies of the former Thyssen Konzern, which now belonged to Vestag. This was particularly true in the trade and transport sectors. Thyssen-Bornemisza understood that his trading and transport companies and gas business had been aligned with Thyssen'sche Hüttenwerke and other companies of the former Thyssen group, which were now part of Vereinigte Stahlwerke. Now the company had to set up its own gas production facilities, apart from the latter, for sales to private and public customers. For this purpose, he sought long-term cooperations.[11] He also had to reckon with the following question: would the traditional organizational and personnel structure of autonomous yet closely cooperating individual companies be viable in the new group?

Bank voor Handel en Scheepvaart N. V. in Rotterdam flourished under its ambitious director Hendrik Jozef Kouwenhoven. He was one of the few senior managers whom Heinrich Thyssen-Bornemisza had not inherited from his father but selected himself. After August Thyssen's death, Thyssen-Bornemisza expanded the bank into a multinational holding company for his investments. In addition to its role as financer of group enterprises, it was a holding company and equity owner of Dutch companies. It became an important hub for capital transfers, etc., for the Thyssens, especially during the Nazi period.

In 1927/28, Thyssen-Bornemisza took control of Berlin-based von der Heydt's Bank, which was suffering from undercapitalization, from his business partner Eduard von der Heydt. The key protagonist was Kouwenhoven, who sought to expand the Bank voor Handel en Scheepvaart into Germany and beyond. Firms and foundations from Thyssen-Bornemisza's field of interest and members of the Thyssen family got involved. The bank's capital stock was substantially increased, and it was housed in a prestigious building at Behrenstrasse 8 in Berlin. As more and more companies from Thyssen-Bornemisza's sphere of influence entered business relations with the bank, the aim was to transform it into a group bank. In 1930, it was renamed August Thyssen-Bank AG. Here, too, the naming attests to the deference for the founding father. It was also symbolic capital, which could be used to attract customers. With the bank's acquisition, the son embraced one of August Thyssen's entrepreneurial maxims. Self-financing had always been a priority for the elder Thyssen, who had no desire to become dependent on a foreign bank. Heinrich Thyssen-Bornemisza filled the supervisory board with relatives, fellow entrepreneurs, and heads of his companies. The bank survived the financial and banking crisis without facing any threat to its existence. It performed "relatively profitably." The hopes for expansion, however, were not fulfilled due to the great economic difficulties at the end of the 1920s and the beginning of the 1930s.[12]

Along with providing support for the corporate group and Thyssen-Bornemisza's risk management, the banking business also performed specific tasks for individual companies. Heinrich Thyssen-Bornemisza and his managers were thus able to expand Thyssen's gas and water works. This undertaking focused on sustainable returns rather than industrial risk. The goal was to win over the municipalities, especially in the Rhineland, as buyers of supply services. In order to have its own source of coal for this purpose, the Walsum coal-mine shaft was established in 1927. However, commissioning was delayed until 1939 for various reasons.[13]

Of the two shipyards belonging to the Thyssen-Bornemisza empire, the Bremen Vulkan company remained "reasonably profitable" during the world economic crisis, while the Flensburg shipbuilding company became a restructuring case.[14]

Heinrich Thyssen-Bornemisza was unable or unwilling to acquire the specialized knowledge for independently analyzing and assessing the respective problems of the group companies. As a result, he usually was unable or unwilling to mediate in conflicts of interest between plant directors. Wixforth vividly elaborates on such cases, which also involved heated disputes within Atunia's board of directors. For example, there were the conflicts between Johann Georg Gröninger (Vulcaan shipping) and Hendrik Jozef Kouwenhoven (BHS), on the one hand, and Matthias Esser, a board member of the financially beleaguered Bremen Vulkan shipyard, on the other. Thyssen-

Bornemisza did not seek to intervene. Wixforth sees the causes of this wait-and-see attitude partly in disinterest, partly in "the inability to mediate conflicts and to set the corporate tone by taking a strategic decision." There were no fundamental corporate decisions to massively expand either the energy industry or the retail and logistics sectors, which were clearly industries of the future. Such shortcomings could be bridged by the banking system, however, as its head Kouwenhoven filled the void left by Heinrich Thyssen-Bornemisza with an ambitious strategy for expansion. Kouwenhoven ignored the expectations of the group and put the concerns of "his" bank (BHS) first. He could do so because the owner gave him room for maneuver—and because he was successful.[15]

Heinrich Thyssen-Bornemisza viewed himself as the keeper of the family tradition. Again, this was evident in his dealings with the corporate structures and the main players, but also in symbolic acts like the choice of the name August Thyssen'sche Unternehmungen des In und Auslandes GmbH to designate his group. It was further manifested in his plans, with his brother Fritz, to erect a large, prestigious administrative building called the August-Thyssen-Haus in Düsseldorf on Königsplatz as a control center for his business legacy. The architecturally sophisticated structure was also intended to house Thyssen-Bornemisza's valuable art collection. Though the planning and preparations for the project, which he obsessed over, took up a great deal of time and energy from around 1927 to 1930, they ultimately fell through.[16] His renaming of von der Heydt's Bank as August Thyssen Bank was similarly a tribute to his father. Such efforts, however, did not go beyond his immediate sphere of influence or attention. Ultimately, having a (August) Thyssen corporate culture in the group's companies did not interest him.

As a businessman, he was not a commercial or political lobbyist in the narrow sense. He was a pensioner and connoisseur who indulged in art collecting and equestrian sports. He was thus the antithesis of his thrifty, ascetic father. By same token, as a networker between Dutch financiers and Rhenish-Westphalian industrialists, he was obviously successful.[17]

In the more immediate corporate context, Heinrich Thyssen-Bornemisza initially sought to merge his heterogeneous companies into a distinct group, a "Baron-Konzern." This name occasionally appears as pragmatic shorthand in the minutes of Atunia's board of directors' meetings.[18] Simultaneously, he wanted to "prove that he could step out of his father's shadow with his own entrepreneurial ideas."[19] Yet he neither realized a group that was conceptually unified with a systematic division of labor nor one whose constituent parts viewed themselves and acted as one group. It remained a mostly disjointed patchwork.

Figure 8.1. Derby, 26 July 1936, Munich. "The Brown Ribbon of Germany." Heinrich Thyssen-Bornemisza holds the winning horse Nereide from his Erlenhof stud farm by the reins. Photo: Alex Menzendorf, Berlin.

The reasons for the conceptual failure in the group's formation have been touched on. Unlike other industrialists such as Hugo Stinnes or Otto Wolff, Heinrich Thyssen-Bornemisza neither forcefully nor doggedly pursued this objective. He soon lost interest, preferring instead to devote his time and energy to other concerns[20] and competencies. Not only did the self-interest of power-conscious and successful plant directors become more apparent, but Thyssen-Bornemisza granted them latitude to thrive. Wixforth describes this as an inverse principal-agent relationship: the principal's function of shaping the company receded, while the plant managers gained in business influence. This was certainly advantageous for the companies, as it increased their opportunities to shape and carry out innovations and investments quickly and efficiently. What's more, as these were generally company managers with a long-standing history with the company, Thyssen benefited.[21]

Despite the futile efforts to centralize and to achieve "sustainable group and synergy effects,"[22] the group prospered overall because the individual businesses did. The causes seem to lie to a large extent in the power of August Thyssen's accumulated portfolio, that is, in the perpetuation of the economic potential, operational structures, and human capital that gave the highly qualified, loyal, experienced, and assured plant directors room to maneuver. "The resulting path dependency," Wixforth notes, "remained a specific feature of the group."[23]

Another feature was the transnational orientation of the "Baron-Konzern." Heinrich continued what his father August Thyssen had started. By 1932, however, according to Wixforth, the group companies were preoccupied with maintaining their competitive position; foreign business was now less significant than it had been at the time of the August Thyssen group. Most likely, it would not have been possible to extend it.

What was new, conversely, was the establishment of the Kaszony Family Foundation in 1926 and—to take care of Heinrich Thyssen-Bornemisza's art collections—the Rohoncz castle family foundation in 1931. These two Swiss foundations were used for asset management and saving taxes. They had no effect on the operations of the group companies.[24] Given the fact that the group did not make any foreign acquisitions until 1932, Wixforth concludes that Thyssen-Bornemisza and its operations directors did not focus on transnational expansion during this period. He estimates that up until 1932 the Heinrich Thyssen-Bornemisza group of companies was "still in a phase of exploration and formation."[25]

Notes

1. Wixforth, *Stahlkonzern*, chap. 2. For the companies and individuals mentioned here and below, see the useful concise identifications in Rasch, *Briefe*, 447–570; also the portraits of group companies in Rasch, "Was wurde aus August Thyssens Firma nach seinem Tod 1926?" 213–332.
2. See the overviews in Gehlen, *Thyssen-Bornemisza-Gruppe*, 33ff. et passim; Wixforth, *Stahlkonzern*, 115–226.
3. Rasch, "August Thyssen und sein Sohn Heinrich," 57 (quote); Wixforth, *Stahlkonzern*, 78–85, 111.
4. Wixforth, *Stahlkonzern*, 91f. (quote).
5. Ibid, 65–75; Derix, *Die Thyssens*, 349–51 (quoting from the foundation charter of 18 December 1926, ibid., 349).
6. Gehlen, *Thyssen-Bornemisza-Gruppe*, 132–48; Derix, *Die Thyssens*, 349–51; Wixforth, *Stahlkonzern*, 65–75, 111.
7. This is discussed in detail in Wixforth, *Stahlkonzern*, 193–221.
8. Rasch, "August Thyssen und sein Sohn Heinrich," 52–53.
9. See the example of the Walsum mine (mine director Wilhelm Roelen), where Thyssen's gas and water works (general director Franz Lenze) was brought to the brink of ruin; Heinrich Thyssen-Bornemisza nevertheless trusted the managers and gave them a free hand; Wixforth, *Stahlkonzern*, 123–31, 221.
10. See below the references to the figures Gehlen obtained on the salary and bonus of Wilhelm Roelen (Thyssengas/Walsum). Such ratios are also likely to have applied during the period under study here.
11. Rasch, "August Thyssen und sein Sohn Heinrich," 54–56.
12. Ibid., 58–62.
13. Rasch, "August und sein Sohn Heinrich," 64f.; Gehlen, *Thyssen-Bornemisza-Gruppe* ; Wixforth, *Stahlkonzern*, 119–34.
14. Wixforth, *Stahlkonzern*, 141–67, 222 (quote), 223.
15. Ibid., 178–221, 223 (quote).
16. See de Taillez, *Bürgerleben*, 111–18; Gramlich, *Kunstsammler*, 204–9; Wixforth, *Stahlkonzern*, 106–8.
17. Wixforth, *Stahlkonzern*, 110. About the interest in art, see Gramlich, *Kunstsammler*.
18. See the reference to the meeting on 22 December 1927 in Urban, *Zwangsarbeit*, 10n8.
19. Wixforth, *Stahlkonzern*, 12.
20. In addition to the interest in art, there was also an increased interest in glamorous social events and racing. In 1933, he acquired the Erlenhof stud farm in Homburg vor der Höhe, including a racing stable in Berlin-Hoppegarten; de Taillez, *Bürgerleben*, 163–70.
21. Wixforth, *Stahlkonzern*, 238–39.
22. Ibid., 226.
23. Ibid., 234–37 (quote 235), 241.
24. Ibid., 6–78, 240; Derix, *Die Thyssens*; Gramlich, *Kunstsammler*.
25. Wixforth, *Stahlkonzern*, 226 (quote), 241.

CHAPTER 9

THE THYSSEN-BORNEMISZA GROUP
A Transnational Business Group in Times of Economic Nationalism, 1932–1955

(Boris Gehlen, 2021)

Gehlen extends Wixforth's period of investigation to 1955, when the German and Dutch companies of the group were demerged in terms of personnel and capital. The Thyssen-Bornemisza transnational alliance thus became two national groups under a single transnational umbrella. This did not change the ownership structure. Heinrich Thyssen-Bornemisza died in 1947, and during his lifetime his son and heir Hans Heinrich Thyssen-Bornemisza had already taken over the management.[1]

For his monograph, Gehlen extensively evaluates sources from private and state archives in Germany, the Netherlands, Great Britain, Switzerland, and the United States. As a result, with the two studies, the history of the Thyssen-Bornemisza group in the period from 1926 to the mid-1950s can be regarded as well researched, and the gap can be considered closed with respect to what we know about the heavy industrial sector of August and Fritz Thyssen.

Boris Gehlen counted seventy-five companies in the Thyssen-Bornemisza group for 1940 ("including twenty-one ships independent under corporate law, a good dozen artificial fertilizer companies and six foreign branches") and found that eleven companies from six sectors made up the group's business core, which, with some qualification, also applied to the year 1926/27:[2]

- Energy, gas, and water: Thyssen'sche Gas und Wasserwerke GmbH
- Steel and machine manufacture: Press- und Walzwerke Reisholz
- Shipbuilding: Bremer Vulkan; Flensburger Schiffsbau-Gesellschaft
- Building materials: Vereinigte Berliner Mörtelwerke AG; Rittergut Rüdersdorf GmbH
- Trade and shipping: N. V. Handels- en Transport Maatschappij Vulcaan; Halcyon Lijn N. V.; N. V. "Vlaardingen-Oost"

- Banks: Bank voor Handel en Scheepvaart; von der Heydt's Bank since 1927/28 (from 1930 onward: August Thyssen Bank).

The group structure was established during the time of inflation. After August Thyssen died, the shareholdings between the heirs were gradually adjusted; the process was completed in 1936 when Hans, Julius, and Fritz Thyssen transferred their shares in the Dutch companies to Thyssen-Bornemisza. In a legal sense, the companies formed a group. They were bound together by the fact that Thyssen-Bornemisza owned all the shares in most of his companies, although in some cases he was "only" the majority shareholder. Formally, the property rights were distributed among different companies. But, as Gehlen discovered, starting in 1936, Heinrich Thyssen-Bornemisza was the beneficial owner, either personally or through the Kaszony Foundation, because he could exercise effective control over the property. The ownership structures were not transparent to third parties as the companies were often intertwined by mutual ownership arrangements and holding companies were also involved. No major corporate shareholdings were acquired until the mid-1950s.

Due to the large number and diversity of these companies, the countries involved, the economic issues, and the differentiation and density of developments during the Nazi period and after the end of the war, it is only possible to highlight the following aspects from the plethora of findings in Boris Gehlen's study.[3]

The involvement of the Thyssen-Bornemisza companies in the armaments industry was consistent with what Urban found in his study of forced labor: the (German) group companies were part of the Nazi arms industry and profited from it. However, unlike some of their competitors, they did not take advantage of the resulting room for maneuver to expand. Their goal was rather to avoid conflict with the regime and get through the war period unscathed. They were not always successful, and there were also conflicts because of the dictates of Nazi economic policy. By the same token, there was no evidence of a corporate policy aimed at working toward or taking advantage of the criminal goals of the Nazi regime.[4]

The transnational organization of the group led to very different constellations and consequences in the upheavals in Europe during the second third of the twentieth century. Depending on the change of national or international economic policy and, of course, on the state interventions during the world war and afterward (confiscation, restitution), it proved to be both a means of protection and a burden. Originally conceived by August and his heirs to protect their assets, manage tax burdens, and diversify, it by no means always lived up to expectations. Especially during the war and in the postwar period, the various states—Germany, the Netherlands, Great Britain, and the United States—had considerable leeway when dealing with the property of Heinrich Thyssen-Bornemisza. He was a German-born Hungarian who, however, lived in Switzerland. With his Swiss Kaszony Foundation, he controlled companies in the Netherlands which, in turn, owned shares in companies in the German Reich and later the Federal Republic and other countries. Finally, he was regarded in the German Reich as *Volksdeutscher* (someone whose language and culture had German origins but was not a German citizen).[5] Thus in restitution claims, the assets of TBG were classified as Dutch in Great Britain and returned, whereas in the United States they were deemed Hungarian or German (because Heinrich Thyssen-Bornemisza was regarded as beneficial owner) and confiscated. TBG lost half of its assets in Canada and all of them in the occupied Soviet zone. By the end of the war, TBG had lost most of its assets (if only temporarily). Thyssen-Bornemisza won the support of the Dutch government, which helped in London, did little or nothing in the United States, and also protected group companies in Germany because they were classified as Dutch property (of the Bank voor Handel en Scheepvaart). Although the "nationality" of a company did not offer lasting protection against state intervention, Gehlen concludes: "Overall ... fluid nationality clearly benefited TBG more than it harmed it."[6]

This political dimension was eclipsed by the economic and business transformation. From the 1940s onward, the German companies in the TBG became less and less important. The group's focus on industry decreased in favor of the financial sector. The securities business had already started to gain significance in the 1920s, up until the spin-off of an investment company from BHS in June 1952. This process only intensified as the relationship between company heir Hans Heinrich Thyssen-Bornemisza and Germany steadily faded. Over the long term, under his leadership, the group divested itself of its German holdings, especially from the 1970s onward. It transformed from a "production-based family group"—i.e., from an organically built-up corporation that seeks to ensure its survival through long-term orientation, diversification, and a clever niche strategy—to a family asset management company. The company continued its traditional industrial activities, such as machine manufacture and the manufacture of pumps and seals, and was also involved in trade (oil), services (information technology), and investment funds.

The group of companies, however, increasingly developed in the direction of a portfolio business group, which is concerned with the optimal use of financial opportunities and risk management. This was becoming a more promising business area. Longer term, and in the context of increased globalization, this contributed to the emergence of TBG from BHS in 1971. The group was restructured in 1974: Hans Heinrich founded a Luxembourg company modeled on the Dutch Holland-American Investment Corporation (HAIC), which had managed the family's holdings. The family assets were transferred to this company, which then set up a corresponding company in the Dutch Antilles, where corporate income tax was extremely low. In 1978, also primarily for tax reasons, Favorita Holding Company Ltd. was founded on the Bermuda Islands, where the company was tax-exempt.[7]

But there were also continuities. For instance, wherever possible, financing was not obtained from outside banks in order to prevent them from gaining influence over the business. Instead, the TBG companies relied on self-financing and the use of the two banks in the network—BHS and ATB— which had different profiles. They also embarked on the path of cross-financing, whereby profitable group companies financed group companies seeking capital. This path also involved shifting entanglements. Long term, TBG pursued a rather moderate dividend policy and was oriented toward achieving future sustainability instead of short-term profit—a typical behavior of family businesses.

Even after 1932, Heinrich Thyssen-Bornemisza maintained the company policy of giving senior directors a great deal of independence and room for maneuver. They were measured by their success and paid handsomely. In this regard, Gehlen managed to find sources for some of the senior TB managers (which is rare), especially for Kouwenhoven and Wilhelm Roelen, general director of Thyssen's gas and water works since 1937, general director of all German (and Dutch) plants of TBG from 1939, and general agent of Heinrich Thyssen-Bornemisza. For the years 1935 to 1952, Gehlen can therefore quantify the ratio of basic salary, expense allowance, and bonus, plus the rent-free company apartment and income from supervisory board mandates. The bonus—and thus the performance-related component—usually accounted for the bulk of the manager's income.[8]

August Thyssen had already introduced a comprehensive information system for measuring, monitoring, and controlling the performance of the individual companies, i.e., a structured financial reporting system that allowed him to meticulously record and compare costs and earnings. Heinrich Thyssen-Bornemisza continued this and expanded on it, with accounting being regarded as the hallmark of modern business management. To this end, he used Rotterdamsch Trustee's Kantoor (RTK), which effectively became TBG's information center. As Gehlen summarizes: "Decentralization, management decision-making autonomy, performance-related compensation and control by accounting were therefore the key principles of management control in the (old) Thyssen group. But they were also suited to lead a business group."[9]

As for the development of TBG in the second third of the twentieth century, Gehlen observes that Heinrich Thyssen-Bornemisza and his son Hans

Heinrich were "not typical entrepreneurs of their time"; TBG, moreover, was not a "typical company but as a business group a special case." Even as it developed into a portfolio group that operated the investment business and became Europeanized and globalized, it remained family owned.[10]

Notes

1. He had disinherited his eldest son, Stephen, who had married against his will. The new head of the multinational group of companies was his youngest son, Hans Heinrich Thyssen-Bornemisza, born in 1921.
2. Gehlen, *Thyssen-Bornemisza-Gruppe*, 33–35 (quote 33) and its fig. 1. For details of the companies, see Wixforth, *Stahlkonzern*, 115–226.
3. See also Gehlen, *Thyssen-Bornemisza-Gruppe*, 400–405.
4. On the acquisition of the previously "Aryanized" Erlenhof stud by the Hollandsch Trustkantoor, see Derix, *Die Thyssens*; also Gehlen, *Thyssen-Bornemisza-Gruppe*, 323–32.
5. See Gehlen, *Thyssen-Bornemisza-Gruppe*, 399.
6. Ibid., 122.
7. Ibid., 110–15 (quote 111).
8. See, in detail, ibid., 152–59.
9. Ibid., 152; see also the references there to Fear, *Organizing Control*.
10. Gehlen, *Thyssen-Bornemisza-Gruppe*, 405.

APPENDIX

THE THYSSEN FAMILY

THE THYSSEN FAMILY TREE

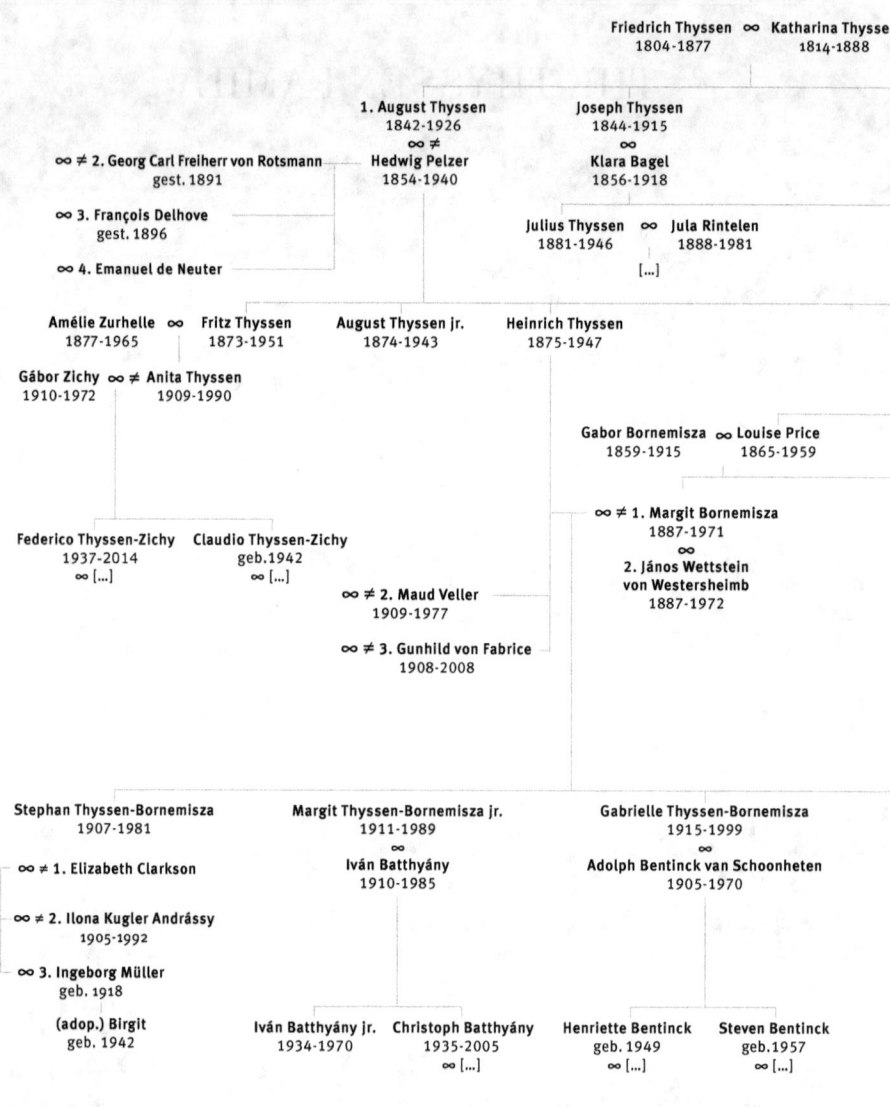

Tree Legend:
adop. = adopted
gest. = died
geb. = born
n. = after

∞ married ≠ divorced
1st/2nd/3rd number of marriages
[...] not listed by name
Spouse without children
© Research: Simone Derix

APPENDIX

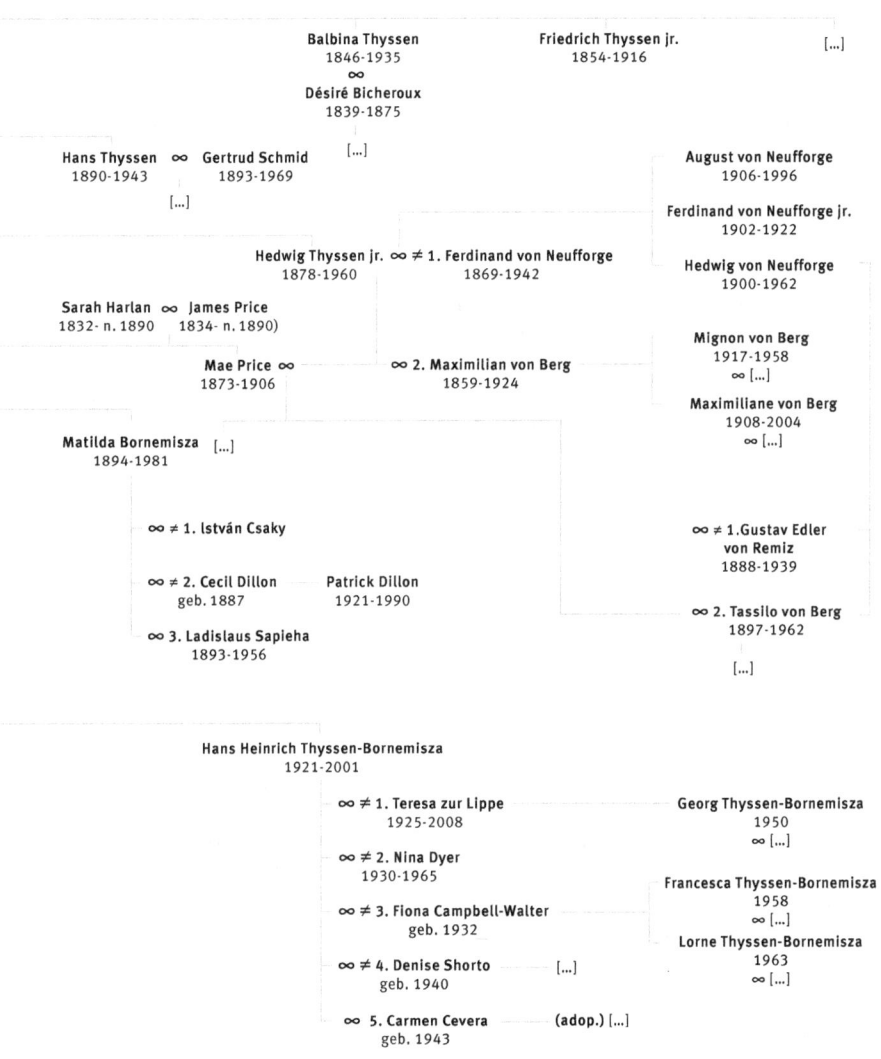

BIBLIOGRAPHY

Bähr, Johannes. *Thyssen in der Adenauerzeit: Konzernbildung und Familienkapitalismus*. Paderborn, 2015.

———. *Werner Siemens: 1816–1892*. Munich, 2016.

Berghahn, Volker. *Hans-Günther Sohl als Stahlunternehmer und Präsident des Bundesverbandes der Deutschen Industrie 1906–1989*. Göttingen, 2020.

Berghoff, Hartmut. *Moderne Unternehmensgeschichte: Eine themen- und theorieorientierte Einführung*. Paderborn, etc., 2004 (2nd ed. 2016).

Berghoff, Hartmut, and Ingo Köhler. *Verdienst und Vermächtnis: Familienunternehmen in Deutschland und den USA seit 1800*. Frankfurt am Main/New York, 2020.

Berghoff, Hartmut, and Jakob Vogel (eds.). *Wirtschaftsgeschichte als Kulturgeschichte: Dimensionen eines Perspektivenwechsels*. Frankfurt am Main/New York, 2004.

Binner, Jens. Review of Thomas Urban. *H-Soz-Kult*, 15 July 2016. Retrieved 2 April 2021 from https://www.hsozkult.de/publicationreview/id/reb-21314.

Brakelmann, Günter. *Zwischen Mitschuld und Widerstand: Fritz Thyssen und der Nationalsozialismus*. Essen, 2020.

Borenius, Tancred (ed.). *Haus Thyssen: Die Sammlung*. Berlin, 1926 (private print).

Bourdieu, Pierre. *Die verborgenen Mechanismen der Macht. Schriften zu Politik und Kultur 1*, ed. Margareta Steinrücke. Hamburg, 1992 (new ed. 2005).

Casson, Mark. *The Entrepreneur: An Economic Theory*. 2nd ed. Cheltenham/Northampton, 2003.

Chandler, Alfred D. *Strategy and Structure: Chapters in the History of the Industrial Enterprise*. Cambridge, MA, 1962.

———. *The Visible Hand: The Managerial Revolution in American Business*. Cambridge, MA, 1977.

———. *Scale and Scope: The Dynamics of Industrial Capitalism*. Cambridge, MA, 1990.

Cohen, Yves. "Les Chefs, une question pour l'histoire du XXe siècle." In *Cités*, no. 6 (2001): 67–83.

———. *Le Siècle des chefs: Une histoire transnationale du commandement et de l'autorité (1890–1940)*. Paris 2013.

Derix, Simone. "Transnationale Familien." In *Dimensionen internationaler Geschichte*, eds. Jost Dülffer and Wilfried Loth, 335–51. Munich, 2012.

———. "Familiale Distanzen: Räumliche Entfernung, ethnische und nationale Zugehörigkeit und Verwandtschaft." *Historische Anthropologie* 22 (2014): 45–66.

———. "Das Rennpferd: Historische Perspektiven auf Zucht und Führung seit dem 18. Jahrhundert." *Body Politics* 2, no. 4 (2014): 397–429.

———. *Die Thyssens: Familie und Vermögen*. Paderborn, 2016 (2nd ed. 2021).

———. "Grenzenloses Vermögen: Räumliche Mobilität und die Infrastrukturen des Reichtums als Zugänge zur historischen Erforschung des 'einen Prozent.'" In Gajek, Kurr, and Seegers, *Reichtum*, 164–81.

Donges, Alexander. *Die Vereinigte Stahlwerke AG im Nationalsozialismus: Konzernpolitik zwischen Marktwirtschaft und Staatswirtschaft*. Paderborn, 2014.
Eglau, Hans Otto. *Fritz Thyssen: Hitlers Gönner und Geisel*. Berlin, 2003.
Ellerbrock, Karl-Peter. Review of Harald Wixforth. *Zeitschrift für Unternehmensgeschichte* 65 (2020): 326f.
Fear, Jeffrey. *Organizing Control: August Thyssen and the Construction of German Corporate Management*. Cambridge/London, 2005.
Ferguson, Niall. *Die Geschichte der Rothschilds: Propheten des Geldes*. Munich/Stuttgart, 2002.
Finger, Jürgen. "Reiche Lebenswelten in NS-Deutschland: Gestaltungschancen vermögender Unternehmerfamilien am Beispiel Dr. Oetker/Richard Kaselowsky." In Gajek, Kurr, and Seegers, *Reichtum*, 77–97.
Finger, Jürgen, Sven Keller, and Andreas Wirsching. *Dr. Oetker und der Nationalsozialismus: Geschichte eines Familienunternehmens 1933–1945*. Munich, 2013.
Föllmer, Moritz. *Individuality and Modernity in Berlin: Self and Society from Weimar to the Wall*. Cambridge et al., 2013.
———. "Wie kollektivistisch war der Nationalsozialismus? Zur Geschichte der Individualität zwischen Weimarer Republik und Nachkriegszeit." In *Kontinuitäten und Diskontinuitäten: Der Nationalsozialismus in der Geschichte des 20. Jahrhunderts*, eds. Birthe Kundrus and Sybille Steinbacher, 30–52. Göttingen 2013.
Gajek, Eva Maria, and Anne Kurr: "Reichtum und Reiche in Deutschland: Neue Perspektiven auf Akteure, Räume, Repräsentationen und Vermessungen im 20. Jahrhundert." In *Reichtum*, eds. Gajek, Kurr, and Seegers, 9–31.
Gajek, Eva Maria, Anne Kurr, and Lu Seegers (Eds.). *Reichtum in Deutschland: Akteure, Räume und Lebenswelten im 20. Jahrhundert*. Göttingen, 2019.
Gehlen, Boris. *Die Thyssen-Bornemisza-Gruppe: Eine transnationale business group in Zeiten des Wirtschaftsnationalismus (1932–1955)*. Paderborn, 2021.
Gomoll, Matthias: Review of Thomas Urban. *Zeitschrift für Unternehmensgeschichte* 61 (2016): 238f.
Gramlich, Johannes. *Die Thyssens als Kunstsammler: Investition und symbolisches Kapital (1900–1970)*. Paderborn, 2015 (2nd ed. 2021).
Grimm, Friedrich. *Der Mainzer Kriegsgerichtsprozess gegen die rheinisch-westfälischen Bergwerksvertreter: Fritz Thyssen, Generaldirektor Kesten, Generaldirektor Wüstenhöfer, Generaldirektor Tengelmann, Bergassessor Olfe, Generaldirektor Spindler*. Berlin, 1923.
———. (Jurist, 1888–1959), Wikipedia. Accessed 13 March 2015 from http://de.wikipedia.org/wiki/Friedrich_Grimm_ percent28Jurist percent29.
Guilbaut, Serge. *How New York Stole the Idea of Modern Art: Abstract Expressionism, Freedom and the Cold War*. Chicago/London, 1983.
Hassler, Uta, Norbert Nußbaum, and Werner Plumpe (eds.). *Ein Unternehmer und sein Haus: August Thyssen und Schloss Landsberg*. Darmstadt, 2013.
Hockerts, Hans Günter. *Ein Erbe für die Wissenschaft: Die Fritz Thyssen Stiftung in der Bonner Republik*. Paderborn, 2018 (2nd ed. 2021).
Knoch, Habbo. *Grandhotels: Luxusräume und Gesellschaftswandel in New York, London und Berlin um 1900*. Göttingen, 2016.
Koch, Elizabeth. "§§ 1626, 1627, 1629: Inhaber der elterlichen Sorge." In *Historisch-kritischer Kommentar zum BGB*. Vol. IV: *Familienrecht, §§ 1297–1921*, eds. Mathias Schmoeckel, Joachim Rückert, and Frank L. Schäfer, 1210–15. Tübingen, 2018.

Köhler, Ingo. "Vernetzter Reichtum: Sozialstrategien und Transnationalität der Privatbankiers im langen 19. Jahrhundert." In *Reichtum*, eds. Gajek, Kurr, Seegers, 57–76.
Kopper, Christopher. Review of Simone Derix. *Historische Zeitschrift* 305 (2017): 599f.
Lesczenski, Jörg. *August Thyssen 1842–1926: Lebenswelt eines Wirtschaftsbürgers*. Essen, 2008.
———. "Aufstieg eines Wirtschaftsbürgers: Der Lebensweg August Thyssens bis zum Ersten Weltkrieg." In *Unternehmer*, eds. Hassler, Nußbaum, and Plumpe, 55–117.
———. Review of Felix de Taillez. *H-Soz-Kult*, 10 May 2018. Retrieved 26 April 2021 from https://www.hsozkult.com/publicationreview/id/reb-24079.
Litchfield, David R. L., in collaboration with Caroline Schmitz. *Die Thyssen-Dynastie: Die Wahrheit hinter dem Mythos*. Oberhausen, 2008 (original Engl. edition 2006).
Macho, Thomas. "Einleitung." In *Das Buch von Rat und Tat: Ein Lesebuch aus drei Jahrtausenden*, ed. Gerd Prechtl, 16–31. Munich, 1999.
Nipperdey, Thomas. *Deutsche Geschichte 1866–1918*. Vol. 1: *Arbeitswelt und Bürgergeist*. Munich, 1990. Vol. 2: *Machtstaat vor der Demokratie*. Munich, 1992.
Plumpe, Werner. *Unternehmensgeschichte im 19. und 20. Jahrhundert*. Boston/Berlin, 2018.
Rabe, Paul-Moritz. "Hauptstadt im Galopp: Das 'Braune Band' als städtisches Prestigeprojekt." In Szöllösi-Janze (ed.): *München*, 169–95.
Rasch, Manfred. "Vom geplanten Bau eines Denkmals für August Thyssen in Hamborn." *Duisburger Forschungen* 45 (2000): 283–311.
———. "August Thyssen und sein Sohn Heinrich Baron Thyssen-Bornemisza: Die zweite und dritte Unternehmergeneration Thyssen." In idem, *Briefe*, 9–78.
———. "Was wurde aus August Thyssens Firma nach seinem Tod 1926?" In Wegener, *August und Joseph Thyssen*, 213–332.
Rasch, Manfred (ed.). *August Thyssen und Heinrich Thyssen-Bornemisza: Briefe einer Industriellenfamilie 1919–1926*. Essen, 2010.
Rasch, Manfred, and Gerald D. Feldman (eds.): *August Thyssen und Hugo Stinnes: Ein Briefwechsel 1898–1922, bearb. und annotiert von Vera Schmidt*. Munich, 2003.
Reckendrees, Alfred. *Das "Stahltrust"-Projekt: Die Gründung der Vereinigte Stahlwerke A.G. und ihre Unternehmensentwicklung 1926–1933/34*. Munich, 2000.
Schäfer, Michael. *Familienunternehmen und Unternehmerfamilien: Zur Sozial- und Wirtschaftsgeschichte der sächsischen Unternehmer 1850–1940*. Munich, 2007.
Schanetzky, Tim. Review of Alexander Donges. *H-Soz-Kult*, 13 August 2015. Retrieved 2 April 2021 from http:// hsozkult.geschichte.hu-berlin.de/rezensionen/2015-3-107.
Schleusener, Jan. *Die Enteignung Fritz Thyssens: Vermögensentzug und Rückerstattung*. Paderborn, 2018.
Schulz, Andreas: Review of Johannes Gramlich. *Vierteljahrschrift für Sozial- und Wirtschaftsgeschichte* 103 (2013): 380f.
Sommer, Manfred. *Sammeln: Ein philosophischer Versuch*. Frankfurt, 1999.
Stiftung Familienunternehmen (ed.). *Die Volkswirtschaftliche Bedeutung der Familienunternehmen*. 5th ed. Munich, 2019.
Szöllösi-Janze, Margit (ed.). *München im Nationalsozialismus: Imagepolitik der "Hauptstadt der Bewegung."* Göttingen, 2017.
Taillez, Felix de. *Zwei Bürgerleben in der Öffentlichkeit: Die Brüder Fritz Thyssen und Heinrich Thyssen-Bornemisza*. Paderborn, 2017.

Treue, Wilhelm. *Die Feuer verlöschen nie: August Thyssen-Hütte 1890–1926*. Düsseldorf-Vienna, 1966.
Treue, Wilhelm, and Helmut Uebbing. *Die Feuer verlöschen nie: August Thyssen-Hütte 1926–1966*. Düsseldorf-Vienna, 1969.
Thyssen, Fritz. *I Paid Hitler*. London, 1941, New York/Toronto 1941 (licensed editions in Chile, Brazil, Sweden, Denmark, Argentina, Portugal, Netherlands, Italy 1942–47).
Urban, Thomas. *Zwangsarbeit bei Thyssen: "Stahlverein" und "Baron-Konzern" im Zweiten Weltkrieg*. Paderborn, 2014 (2nd ed. 2021).
Warnke, Martin. "Von der Gegenständlichkeit und der Ausbreitung der Abstrakten." In *Die fünfziger Jahre: Beiträge zu Politik und Kultur*, ed. Dieter Bänsch, 209–22. Tübingen, 1985.
Wegener, Stephan (ed.). *August und Joseph Thyssen: Die Familie und ihre Unternehmen*. 2nd ed. Essen, 2008.
Weniger, Matthias. *Benoit Oppenheim und die Geschichte des Skulpturensammelns in Deutschland: Exposé des Habilitationsprojekts*. LMU Munich, 2018.
Willems, Marianne. "Individualität: Ein bürgerliches Orientierungsmuster; Zur Epochencharakteristik von Empfindsamkeit und Sturm und Drang." In *Bürgerlichkeit im 18. Jahrhundert*, ed. Hans-Edwin Friedrich, 171–200. Tübingen 2006.
Wixforth, Harald. *Vom Stahlkonzern zum Firmenverbund: Die Unternehmen Heinrich Thyssen-Bornemiszas von 1926 bis 1932*. Paderborn, 2019.
Wörner, Birgit, and Jörg Lesczenski. "Häusliche Geselligkeiten und Lebensstile an Ruhr und Main." In Hassler, Nußbaum, and Plumpe, *Unternehmer*, 447–81.
Württemberg, Alexander von (ed.). *Sammlung Fritz Thyssen: Ausgewählte Meisterwerke*. Munich 1986.

OVERVIEW OF THE BOOK SERIES

The following volumes have been published by Verlag Ferdinand Schöningh, Paderborn, an imprint of the Brill Group, as part of the series "Familie—Unternehmen—Öffentlichkeit: Thyssen im 20. Jahrhundert," edited by Hans Günter Hockerts, Günther Schulz, and Margit Szöllösi-Janze.

Volume 10
Boris Gehlen: *Die Thyssen-Bornemisza-Gruppe: Eine transnationale business group in Zeiten des Wirtschaftsnationalismus (1932–1955)*
1st edition 2021, 445 pp., 26 b&w diag., 17 b&w illus., 31 b&w tabs.
ISBN: 978-3-506-76012-8

Volume 9
Harald Wixforth: *Vom Stahlkonzern zum Firmenverbund: Die Unternehmen Heinrich Thyssen-Bornemiszas von 1926 bis 1932*
1st edition 2019, 269 pp., 12 b&w diag., 1 b&w illus., 3 b&w tabs.
ISBN: 978-3-506-79252-5

Volume 8
Hans Günter Hockerts: *Ein Erbe für die Wissenschaft: Die Fritz Thyssen Stiftung in der Bonner Republik*
2nd edition 2021, 341 pp., 27 b&w illus.
ISBN: 978-3-506-76016-6

Volume 7
Jan Schleusener: *Die Enteignung Fritz Thyssens: Vermögensentzug und Rückerstattung*
1st edition 2018, 261 pp., 10 b&w illus.
ISBN: 978-3-506-78687-6

Volume 6
Felix de Taillez: *Zwei Bürgerleben in der Öffentlichkeit: Die Brüder Fritz Thyssen und Heinrich Thyssen-Bornemisza*
1st edition 2017, 546 pp., 1 b&w diag., 19 b&w illus.
ISBN: 978-3-506-78445-2

Volume 5
Johannes Bähr: *Thyssen in der Adenauerzeit: Konzernbildung und Familienkapitalismus*
1st edition 2015, 211 pp., 1 b&w diag., 19 b&w illus., 13 b&w tabs.
ISBN: 978-3-506-78194-9

Volume 4
Simone Derix: *Die Thyssens: Familie und Vermögen*
2nd edition 2021, 544 pp., 4 b&w diag., 11 b&w illus., 6 b&w tabs.
ISBN: 978-3-506-76060-9

Volume 3
Johannes Gramlich: *Die Thyssens als Kunstsammler: Investition und symbolisches Kapital (1900–1970)*
2nd edition 2021, 428 pp., 1 diag., 12 b&w illus.
ISBN: 978-3-506-77981-6

Volume 2
Thomas Urban: *Zwangsarbeit bei Thyssen: "Stahlverein" und "Baron-Konzern" im Zweiten Weltkrieg*
2nd edition 2021, 197 pp., 15 b&w illus., 9 tab.
ISBN: 978-3-506-76044-9

Volume 1
Alexander Donges: *Die Vereinigte Stahlwerke AG im Nationalsozialismus: Konzernpolitik zwischen Marktwirtschaft und Staatswirtschaft*
1st edition 2014, 440 pp., 30 diag., 60 tab.
ISBN: 978-3-506-76628-1

INDEX

Adenauer, Konrad, 35, 70, 110–11, 113
Aken, Robert van, 34
Arnold, Karl, 113

Bähr, Johannes, 35, 105, 108, 110, 113
Batthyány, Iván, 36n2
Batthyány, Margit, 68
Bentinck van Schoonheten, Adolph, vii, 23, 36n2
Bentinck van Schoonheten, Gabrielle, vii, 23, 36n2, 59, 68
Berghoff, Hartmut, xii–xiv
Birrenbach, Kurt, viii, 35–36, 84, 89, 111
Bismarck, Otto von, 60
Blass, Heinrich, 34
Böckler, Hans, 110
Borbet, Walter, ix, 104
Borcke, Adrian von, viii, 51–52
Bornemisza, Adèle, vii, 23
Bornemisza de Kászon, Baron Gábor, viii, 23–24, 36n2
Borenius, Tancred, ix, 62, 66, 71n14
Bosch, Robert, 106
Bourdieu, Pierre, 57
Buchheim, Christoph, xvi, 93–94

Casson, Mark, 82, 109
Chandler, Alfred D., 82
Churchill, Winston, 54
Cohen, Yves, 44
Cook, Thomas, 27

Debeugny, Colonel, viii, 42
Derix, Simone, 4, 7, 11, 13–15, 17–20, 22, 25–26, 30–35, 39, 50, 84
Donges, Alexander, 74, 90, 94–97, 102
Dörnhöffer, Friedrich, 47, 64
Draughn, Marion, 46

Ellscheid, Robert, vii–viii, 5, 35–36, 55, 84, 86, 89, 105, 110–11
Erhard, Ludwig, 113
Erzberger, Matthias, 41
Esser, Matthias, 119

Fabrice, Gunhild von (married Thyssen-Bornemisza), 25
Fear, Jeffrey, xiv
Feller, Maud, (married Thyssen-Bornemisza), viii, 25, 30, 38n36, 47–48
Fernández Pérez, Paloma, xiv
Fleischmann, Ernst August, 64
Flick, Friedrich, 101
Franz Joseph I, Emperor, 23, 80
Fridenson, Patrick, xiii
Friedländer, Max, 64–66

Gajek, Eva Maria, 14
Gaulle, Charles de, ix, 111–12
Geertz, Clifford, xiii
Gehlen, Boris, 31, 35, 49, 74, 80, 83, 117, 124–25, 127
Goergen, Fritz-Aurel, 86, 112–13, 114n4
Göring, Hermann, 45, 51–52, 61, 104
Goudstikker, Eduard, 64
Grabsch, Ernst, viii, 51
Gramlich, Johannes, 11, 19, 57, 59–64, 66–71
Grimm, Friedrich, viii, 42, 44–45, 56n19
Gröninger, Johann Georg, 34, 119

Härle, Carl, 34–35
Harriman, Edward Roland, 32, 34
Hayes, Peter, 93

INDEX

Heimbach, August, 36n2
Heinemann, Rudolf, 47, 64
Herrigel, Gary, xiv
Herzog, Eduard, 100
Heydt, Eduard von der, 64, 119
Heydt, Karl von der, 60
Hitler, Adolf, ix–x, 45, 51, 53–54, 61, 70, 103–5
Hockerts, Hans Günter, xvi–xvii, 17, 35, 69, 78
Hoffmann, Heinrich, ix, 45
Huret, Jules, 60

Jacke, Fritz, 34–35

Kabelac, Robert, 101
Kaselowsky, Richard, 50, 56n30
Kesten, Wilhelm, 55nn9–10
Knoch, Habbo, 22
Köhler, Ingo, xiv, 30
Koselleck, Reinhart, 40
Kouwenhoven, Hendrik Jozef, 34–35, 38n66, 86, 117–20, 127
Krupp von Bohlen und Halbach, Gustav, 44
Kurr, Anne, 14

Lehr, Robert, 47
Lenbach, Franz von, 60
Lenze, Franz, 118, 123n9
Lesczenski, Jörg, 20, 73
Lievense, Cornelis, 34
Lubinski, Christina, xiv
Lübke, Heinrich, 70

Macho, Thomas, 6
Mann, Erika, 27
Mann, Klaus, 27
Mann, Thomas, 54
Margaret of York, Princess, 70
McCloy, John J., 110

Nipperdey, Thomas, 15

Olfe, Hermann, 55nn9–10
Oppenheimer, James Moritz, 49

Pelzer, Hedwig (married Thyssen) *see* Thyssen, Hedwig
Pferdmenges, Robert, 35, 84, 86–87, 89, 110–12, 114n4, 114n16
Price, Louise (married Bornemisza), 63
Prinz, Michael, xiv

Rasch, Manfred, xvii, 73
Rauschning, Hermann, 54
Reckendrees, Alfred, 94
Reusch, Paul, 101
Reves, Emery, 54–55, 104
Rilke, Rainer Maria, 60
Rodin, Auguste, ix, 60–61, 63
Roelen, Wilhelm, 34, 98, 101, 123n9, 123n9–10, 127
Rothschild, Mayer Amschel, 82–83

Sabean, David, xi, 32
Scherner, Jonas, 93
Schlageter, Albert Leo, 45
Schleusener, Jan, 33, 53, 105–6
Schömann, Minna, vii, 13, 37n3
Schröder, Gerhard, 113
Schulz, Günther, x–xi, xiii, xvi–xvii
Scranton, Philip, xiii
Siemens, Carl von, 83
Siemens, Werner von, 83
Siemens, Wilhelm, 83
Sohl, Hans-Günther, vii–viii, ix, 5, 35–36, 84–87, 89, 110–13
Sommer, Manfred, 57
Spindler, Walter, 55nn9–10
Stinnes, Hugo, 44, 122
Szöllösi-Janze, Margit, x–xi, xiii, xvi–xvii

Taillez, Felix de, 11, 39, 40–41, 43–47, 49, 53–55
Temin, Peter, 93
Tengelmann, Ernst, viii, 42, 55n9
Terboven, Josef, 45, 53
Teresa zur Lippe, Princess, vii, 12
Thyssen, Amélie (née Zurhelle), vii–viii, ix–x, 5, 14, 17, 21, 26–28, 35–36, 46, 53, 55, 58, 62, 69, 78, 84–87, 89, 104, 106, 108–13, 114n6, 114n16

Thyssen, Anita (married Zichy), 17, 21, 33, 78, 84, 87, 89, 108, 110–11, 114n6

Thyssen, August Sr., vii, x–xi, xvi, 1–3, 7, 12–18, 20–22, 26–27, 30–32, 34–35, 36n2, 37n3, 39–41, 43, 49, 59–61, 66, 73–74, 77, 80, 83–84, 87, 115, 117–18, 122, 125, 127

Thyssen, August Jr., vii, 2–3, 13, 15, 18, 21–23, 27, 30–31, 35, 38n45, 91n2

Thyssen, Fritz, vii–xi, 2–3, 5, 7, 11, 13–15, 17–18, 21–22, 26–28, 30–33, 35, 36n2, 38n46, 38n49, 39–46, 49, 53–55, 55n10, 58–59, 61–64, 66, 73–75, 78, 81, 84, 87–89, 95–97, 101, 103–6, 108–9, 111, 115–16, 120, 125

Thyssen, Hans, 31, 38n60, 106, 116, 125

Thyssen, Hedwig (née Pelzer), vii, 2–3, 14–15, 21, 33, 37n3, 74

Thyssen, Hedwig („Hede"), vii, 2–3, 13, 15, 35, 80, 92n2

Thyssen, Joseph, 2, 30–31, 38n60, 106

Thyssen, Julius, 31, 38n60, 106, 116, 125

Thyssen-Bornemisza, Carmen, 59

Thyssen-Bornemisza, Georg Heinrich, xvi–xvii, 80

Thyssen-Bornemisza, Hans Heinrich, vii, 12, 18–19, 30, 37n3, 63, 67–70, 72n27, 80, 88, 90, 124, 126–28

Thyssen(-Bornemisza), Heinrich, vii–ix, xi, 2–4, 11, 13, 15, 18, 22–27, 29–32, 35, 36n2, 37n3, 38n38, 38n46, 38n49, 39–40, 46–47, 49–52, 62–68, 70, 73–74, 80–82, 86, 88–90, 97–98, 101, 115–22, 123n9, 124–27

Thyssen-Bornemisza, Margit (née Bornemisza, remarried Wettstein von Westersheimb), vii–viii, 18, 23, 25, 29, 36n2, 37n3, 46

Thyssen-Bornemisza, Stephan, viii, 29, 68, 90, 128n1

Urban, Thomas, 52, 74, 97–102, 125

Vögler, Albert, ix, 104
Veblen, Thorstein, 20

Weber, Christian, viii, 50, 52
Weniger, Matthias, 62
Wettstein von Westersheimb, János, vii, 18, 23, 36n2
Wilhelm I, II, Emperors, 60
Winterhalder, Baron Guillermo von, 110–11
Winterhoff, Fritz, 101
Wixforth, Harald, 31, 74, 80, 83, 115, 119–20, 122
Wolff, Otto, 122
Wüstenhöfer, Franz, viii, 42, 55n9

Zichy-Thyssen, Anita *see* Thyssen, Anita
Zichy-Thyssen, Claudio, 17, 88
Zichy-Thyssen, Federico, 17, 88

www.ingramcontent.com/pod-product-compliance
Lightning Source LLC
Chambersburg PA
CBHW072056110526
44590CB00018B/3191